West Coast Plays

WITHDRAWN

Available:

West Coast Plays 1 (Fall 1977)

David Rudkin's *Ashes*   •   Susan Miller's *Cross Country*
Douglas Gower's *Daddies*   •   Steven Yafa's *Passing Shots*

West Coast Plays 2 (Spring 1978)

Robert Gordon's *And*
Michael McClure's *Goethe: Ein Fragment*
Louis Phillips' *The Last of the Marx Brothers' Writers*
John Robinson's *Wolves*

West Coast Plays 3 (Fall 1978)

Robert Eisele's *Animals Are Passing from Our Lives*
Nicholas Kazan's *Safe House*   •   J. Paul Porter's *St. George*
Susan Rivers' *Maud Gonne Says No to the Poet*
William Whitehead's *And If That Mockingbird Don't Sing*

West Coast Plays 4 (Spring 1979)

Adele Edling Shank's *Sunset /Sunrise*   •   Ted Pezzulo's *Skaters*
Madeline Puccioni's *Two O'Clock Feeding*
Albert Innaurato's *Earth Worms*

West Coast Plays 5 (Fall 1979)

Robert Patrick's *Judas*   •   Lisa Shipley's *The Bathtub*
Nancy Larson's *Imitations*
Martin Epstein's *Autobiography of a Pearl Diver*

West Coast Plays 6 (Spring 1980)

Michele Linfante's *Pizza*
Glenn Hopkins and Wayne Lindberg's *Dinosaur*
Michael Lynch's *Sylvester the Cat vs. Galloping Billy Bronco*
Barbara Graham's *Jacob's Ladder*

Order from:
West Coast Plays, P.O. Box 7206, Berkeley, CA 94707
$5 each (add 6% sales tax if ordered in California)

Contents

The Chicago Conspiracy Trial was first produced at the Odyssey Theatre, Los Angeles, on March 6, 1979, with the following cast:

COURT; JUDGE JULIUS HOFFMAN	George Murdock
DAVID DELLINGER, *defendant*	Logan Ramsey
RENNIE DAVIS, *defendant*	Dan Mason
TOM HAYDEN, *defendant*	Lance Rosen
ABBIE HOFFMAN, *defendant*	Paul Lieber
JERRY RUBIN, *defendant*	Karl Gregory Clemens
LEE WEINER, *defendant*	Lonnie Ellison
JOHN FROINES, *defendant*	John Ellis
BOBBY SEALE, *defendant*	Leopoldo Mandeville
WILLIAM M. KUNSTLER, *defense*	Lev Mailer
LEONARD WEINGLASS, *defense*	Kenneth Tigar
STEWART ALBERT, *defense*	Stan Roth
THOMAS AQUINAS FORAN, *prosecution*	Hal Bokar
RICHARD G. SCHULTZ, *prosecution*	Tom Bower
KRISTI A. KING, *juror*	Dena Lesser
RUTH L. PETERSON, *juror*	Joan Blair
DAVID E. STAHL, *witness*	John Christy Ewing
SGT. BAILEY/MAYOR RICHARD DALEY	Marty Davis
BARBARA BRADDOCK, *witness*	D. J. Sydney
ROBERT CONNELLY/ROBERT PETERSON	John Darrah
WILLIAM ALBRIGHT, *witness*	John W. Davis
RICHARD GRANDHOLM/JAMES B. HATLEN	Robert Alan Browne
ALLEN GINSBERG, *witness*	Hal Schwartz
MICHELLE DELLINGER, *spectator*	Martina Fink
JEFF MILLER, *spectator*	Steve Tracy
SHARON, *Weiner's girlfriend*	Robin Ginsburg
SUSAN, *Davis's girlfriend*	Janice Galloway Dow
TOM GRACE, *spectator*	Ed Levey
U.S. MARSHAL DON DOBROWSKI	Kenneth Dobbs
SEALE'S CUSTODIAN	Randy Johnson
COURT REPORTER	Lou Hancock
MARSHALS	John Sammon, David Watkins, Joshua Cadman

Directed by Frank Condon
Set design by Leonard A. Felix
Sound by Hal Schwartz
Lighting by Ana Oakes
Media by Rob Reed
Properties by Nancy Frey
Costumes coordinated by Kim Simons

SETTING

The United States Courthouse, Chicago, Illinois. September 1969 through February 1970.

HAYDEN: It implied no disrespect for the jury; it is my customary greeting.

COURT: Regardles of what it implies, sir, there will be no fist shaking and I caution you not to repeat it. That applies to all the defendants, Mr. Schultz.

SCHULTZ: In promoting and encouraging this riot, the three men whom I just mentioned used an organization which they called the National Mobilization Committee to End the War in Vietnam to plan these activities. Two of these defendants, the defendant Abbie Hoffman who sits—who is just standing for you, ladies and gentlemen . . .

COURT: The jury is directed to disregard the kiss thrown by the defendant Hoffman and the defendant is directed not to do that sort of thing again.

SCHULTZ: . . . and with them a man named Jerry Rubin who is standing there—these two men called themselves leaders of the Yippies.

HOFFMAN AND RUBIN: Yippie!

COURT: Contempt of court is any act calculated to hinder or disrupt the Court in its administration of justice. Mr. Schultz.

SCHULTZ: Two more of these individuals, Lee Weener who is a research . . .

WEINER: Weiner.

SCHULTZ: . . . Lee Weiner, who just stood, who is a research assistant—calls himself a professor of sociology at Northwestern University, and John Froines . . . He is an assistant professor of chemistry at the University of Oregon. Weener and Froines joined . . .

WEINER: Weiner.

SCHULTZ: . . . joined with Davis, Dellinger and Hayden. And the eighth person who joined is a man named Bobby Seale, seated at the end of the table. Ladies and gentlemen of the jury, we will prove that each of these eight men assumed specific roles, and that the plans to incite the riot were basically in three steps. The first step was to use the unpopularity of the war in Vietnam as a method to urge people to come to Chicago during that convention for purposes of protest. The second step was to incite these people against the police department, the city officials, the National Guard, and the military, and against the convention itself, so that these people would physically resist and defy the orders of the police and the military. The third step was to create a situation where the demonstrators who had come to Chicago and were conditioned physically to resist the police, would meet and would confront the police in the streets of Chicago so that at the confrontation a riot would occur.

In sum then, ladies and gentlemen, the Government will prove that the eight defendants charged here conspired together to use the facilities of interstate commerce to incite and further a riot in Chicago; that they conspired to use incendiary devices to further that riot and they conspired to have people interfere with law enforcement officers, and that the defendants committed overt acts in the furtherance of this conspiracy. Ladies and gentlemen of the jury, the Government will prove each of these eight defendants guilty as charged.

COURT: Is it the desire of any lawyer of a defendant to make an opening statement?

KUNSTLER: It is, Your Honor.

COURT: All right. You may proceed, Mr. Kunstler.

KUNSTLER: Ladies and gentlemen of the jury. We hope to prove before you that this prosecution which you are hearing is the result of two motives on the part of the Government...

SCHULTZ: Objection as to any motives of the Prosecution, if the Court please.

KUNSTLER: Your Honor, it is a proper defense to show motive.

COURT: I sustain the objection. You may speak of the guilt or innocence of your clients, not to the motive of the Government.

KUNSTLER: Your Honor, I have always thought that...

SCHULTZ: Objection to any colloquies, and arguments, Your Honor.

COURT: I sustain the objection, regardless of what you have always thought, Mr. Kunstler.

KUNSTLER: The Defense will show that the real conspiracy in this case is the conspiracy to curtail and prevent the demonstrations against the war in Vietnam and related issues; that these defendants and other people, thousands, who came here were determined to influence the delegates of a political party meeting in Chicago; that the real conspiracy was against these defendants. But we are going to show that the real conspiracy is not against these defendants as individuals, because they are unimportant as individuals. The real attempt was—the real attack was on the rights of everybody, all of us American citizens, all, to protest against a war that was brutalizing, is brutalizing, us all, and to

discontinue questioning in this case, because now the Court has revealed the letter.

COURT: The objections of the Government will be sustained and the motion denied. Under the circumstances I have no alternative, since the juror has said that having seen this letter, she cannot function fairly and impartially as a juror. You are excused from further service, Miss King. Mr. Marshal, let me have the first alternate juror's card.

KUNSTLER: Your Honor, I think the interrogation should go further here. She should be questioned as to her knowledge of the Panthers, what they are, what her thoughts are, and so on.

COURT: The Panthers aren't indicted here, sir. I am not trying the Panthers. I know nothing about them.

SEALE: But I am a member of the Panther Party.

KUNSTLER: We think they are indicted, Your Honor, in the eyes of the public.

COURT: Mr. Marshal, will you please instruct that defendant to remain quiet during this discussion.

WEINGLASS: If the Court please, may I just be heard on a point of law with respect to this matter. The United States Supreme Court has recently handed down . . .

COURT: I will not interrogate this juror as to her knowledge of this—what do they call it—the Black Panthers, if indeed, such an organization exists—and I don't know whether it does, I am not trying any organization here; I am trying eight individuals.

WEINGLASS: Your Honor . . .

COURT: A juror has the right to say he or she can't be fair. Alternate juror Kay Richards will be substituted for juror Kristi A. King. You are Ruth L. Peterson.

MRS. PETERSON: Yes.

COURT: The marshal is handing you Government's Exhibit B-2 for identification. Will you please tell the court whether or not you have ever seen this before?

MRS. PETERSON: Yes. We received this in the mail—when was it? Monday.

COURT: When you say "we," you mean your family?

MRS. PETERSON: My family, yes.

COURT: Having seen that letter, do you still feel that you can continue to be a fair and impartial juror?

MRS. PETERSON: Yes.

COURT: And that you can give these eight defendants as well as the United States of America . . .

MRS. PETERSON: Yes, I do.

COURT: ... a fair and impartial trial?

MRS. PETERSON: Yes.

COURT: You do?

MRS. PETERSON: Yes. I think it is my duty to.

COURT: This juror will be permitted to remain on the jury.

KUNSTLER: Your Honor, the defendants believe the two letters in question were sent by some agent of the Government in order to prejudice them further in this trial.

COURT: I will let you try to prove that right now. That is a very grave charge against an officer of the Government.

KUNSTLER: Well, we obviously can't prove it, Your Honor.

COURT: Then don't say it.

KUNSTLER: That is my clients' position. That is my statement.

COURT: To make a statement like that is irresponsible.

KUNSTLER: We would hope that Your Honor would set this down for a hearing, so that what Your Honor has termed—and we agree with Your Honor—is a very serious allegation can at last begin to unravel in this courtroom.

FORAN: Your Honor, the Government objects to the totally frivolous, idiotic proposal that you have hearings to determine inferences of possibilities of circumstantial evidence. I wish really— well, Your Honor, the Government objects to it. It is so—I wish the showboat tactics would stop.

COURT: Mr. Marshal, I direct you at an appropriate time after this hearing to see to it that the members of the jury are sequestered, and that the newspapers and other journals and radio and television are kept from them, and any other people who might try to talk with them.

KUNSTLER: Your Honor, the Defense moves for the unsequestration of the jury. We think it is more human.

COURT: I will deny the motion. Assuming there is such a word as— what did you call it?

KUNSTLER: I said "unsequestration," Your Honor. We mean that they should not be locked up during the trial.

COURT: I have treated your motion as such.

CLERK: There is a motion here of defendant Bobby Seale *pro se* to be permitted to defend himself.

COURT: I will hear you, Mr. Seale.

SEALE: I, Bobby Seale, demand and move the Court as follows. Because I am denied the lawyer of my choice, Charles R. Garry, I cannot represent myself as my attorney would be doing. Because

COURT: If the United States Attorney said that, I certainly will. Crowd the "baby" out of your minds. We are not dealing with babies here. Please continue Mr. . . .

WEINGLASS: Weinglass, Your Honor. At the August 7th meeting with Abbie Hoffman and Jerry Rubin did Mr. Hoffman and Mr. Rubin indicate to you that if the Yippies were permitted to stay in the park that everything would be OK and nonviolent?

STAHL: I don't recall words exactly to that effect being—or statements to that effect being made at that meeting.

WEINGLASS: What was the general tenor of their remarks, Mr. Stahl?

STAHL: They opened the meeting by saying they wanted to avoid violence. They also followed that statement subsequently with statements about their willingness to tear up the town and the convention and to die in Lincoln Park.

WEINGLASS: But in between that first statement you made and the second, did they not indicate that if the city would permit them to stay in the parks, that there would be no violence and that everything would be all right?

STAHL: I would suspect they made a statement something along those lines in the course of the meeting.

WEINGLASS: Thank you. I am showing you your handwritten notes of the August 12th meeting, marked Defendants' Exhibit 8. Is that your handwritten note, a copy of it?

STAHL: Yes, these are a copy of my notes of the meeting on August 12th.

WEINGLASS: Directing your attention to the first page, did you state right at the beginning that the National Mobilization Committee made it clear to you at the outset that they wanted to avoid unnecessary tensions, is that correct?

STAHL: Mr. Dellinger made that statement and immediately followed with a statement that he believed in civil disobedience, that he just returned from Paris where he studied police riots. I think that he would say violence and then non-violence and then say . . .

WEINGLASS: Is that correct? Well, does that statement appear in your notes?

STAHL: Yes, the statement about civil disobedience does.

WEINGLASS: Yes, now would you read to the jury, after having said that, what your notes reflect Mr. Dellinger said about civil disobedience?

FORAN: Object to that.

KUNSTLER: If the court please, it is my understanding that there is no constitutional or legal obligation on the part of a defendant to rise so long as his failure to rise is not disruptive.

COURT: You advise your clients not to rise, do you?

KUNSTLER: They are in protest of what you have done to Bobby Seale's right to defend himself.

COURT: Will you advise your clients to rise, Mr. Kunstler?

KUNSTLER: Your Honor, if you direct me to, I will advise them.

COURT: I direct you to.

KUNSTLER: Then I will pass on the direction, but I cannot in good conscience do more than that. They are free and independent and they have to do what they please.

COURT: Let the record show that none of the defendants has risen.

Blackout.

SCENE FIVE

Testimony of Government Witness SERGEANT BAILY
of the Chicago Police Department

SCHULTZ: Would you relate what you heard, please?

BAILY: I heard Mr. Rubin saying that the pigs started the violence, and he says, "Tonight we're not going to give up the park. We have to meet violence." He says, "The pigs are armed with guns and Mace, so we have to arm ourselves with—any kind of weapon they could get."

SCHULTZ: Did he say anything more that you recall? Do you recall any further statements by him at this time?

BAILY: I don't recall what else he said, but he ended up with saying, "And don't forget our gigantic love-in on the beaches tomorrow."

SCHULTZ: When the police car came, the marked police car came behind the barricade, did any of the people turn and face the police car?

BAILY: Yes, they did.

SCHULTZ: Then what occurred, please?

BAILY: Well, they began to throw rocks at it, boards, two-by-fours that were cut in half, hitting the car with it, breaking the windows. One took a piece of board that looked like an axe handle and started swinging at the blue light on the roof. The car went into the barricade and hit the barricade and then backed out and they were yelling, "Kill the pigs. Get them. Get those pigs in the car."

SCHULTZ: After the squad car left the area of the barricade, Sgt. Baily, what occurred?

BAILY: Shortly after, eight to ten patrolmen approached, spread out...

SCHULTZ: And what occurred please?

BAILY: Objects came from the crowd, from behind the barricade again, bricks and stones mostly, bottles and cans, and one policeman turned, started running back, fell down, and they cheered and the policemen retreated.

SCHULTZ: What if anything did Mr. Rubin say during the preceding ten minutes before the policemen were assaulted which would encourage the crowd to assault the policemen?

BAILY: He said, "Let's get the m–f–en pigs out of here." He said, "Take off your guns and we'll fight you," and "you're shitheads," and "you're m–f–s," and "your kids are f–en pigs."

Blackout.

SCENE SIX

Testimony of Government Witness BARBARA BRADDOCK,
a Chicago policewoman

SCHULTZ: Mrs. Braddock, who said, "Another good idea is golf balls"?

BRADDOCK: Abbie Hoffman said, "Another good idea is golf balls, with nails pounded through them in all different angles, so that when you throw them they will stick," and he said, "But don't forget the vaseline for your faces to protect against the Mace, because there's going to be a lot of Mace flying, and don't forget your helmets, because you're going to need them to protect against the pigs." And then someone asked about holding the park that night, and he said, "Yeah, we should hold the park at all costs. It's our park, and the blank pigs have no right to push us out. It's our park and we're going to fight," and at that point my partner and I left.

SCHULTZ: Now did you have occasion to see the defendant Rubin on Monday, August 26, 1968?

BRADDOCK: Yes, he was up on that table again with a megaphone making another speech.

SCHULTZ: Would you relate, please, what you recall of his speech?

BRADDOCK: He screamed into the megaphone, "The pigs aren't going to push us out of the park tonight. Let's get those bloodthirsty blankety-blank pigs."

COURT: I sit in the place where I should sit.

KUNSTLER: While I am standing up.

COURT: I will not permit you to lean on that. If you are tired we can take a recess and you can go to sleep for the afternoon.

KUNSTLER: I am not that tired, Your Honor.

COURT: Then please continue, Mr. Kunstler.

KUNSTLER: Thank you, Your Honor.

COURT: Yes, you're very welcome.

KUNSTLER: Can you describe what Mr. Hayden looked like then?

BRADDOCK: His hair was fairly close to regular length. I don't remember a moustache or anything. Sort of beady eyes.

KUNSTLER: Beady eyes?

BRADDOCK: Yes.

KUNSTLER: You don't like these defendants at all do you?

FORAN: Object to that.

COURT: Objection sustained.

KUNSTLER: Nothing further.

COURT: Is there any redirect?

SEALE: I would like to cross-examine the witness.

COURT: Mr. Seale . . .

SEALE: I want to cross-examine the witness.

COURT: Please be quiet, sir.

SEALE: My constitutional rights have been violated.

COURT: I order you to be quiet.

SEALE: I have a right to cross-examine the witness.

COURT: Now I want to tell you, Mr. Seale, again—you are not to intrude upon these proceedings in an improper manner.

SEALE: I have never intruded until it was the proper time for me to ask . . .

COURT: I must tell you sir, that if you are going to persist in this sort of thing, the Court will have to deal appropriately with your conduct.

Blackout.

SCENE SEVEN

Testimony of Government Witness ROBERT CONNELLY, *Undercover Investigator*

WEINGLASS: As things quieted down, did you see the police form a line?

CONNELLY: The line that I recall seeing had already formed and it was partially into the crowd where the speakers on the microphone systems were telling the crowd to sit down and then as the crowd sat down, the police retreated also.

WEINGLASS: Can you tell the jury in what manner the police came into the crowd? Was there a formation?

CONNELLY: Yes sir, there was.

WEINGLASS: Describe the formation of the police.

CONNELLY: It was a wedge-type formation.

WEINGLASS: How would you describe a wedge-type formation specifically?

CONNELLY: A "V" shape.

WEINGLASS: Were these policemen armed?

CONNELLY: Well, all uniformed police officers are armed.

WEINGLASS: What were they armed with?

CONNELLY: From what I could see they had their standard equipment.

WEINGLASS: Will you describe what they had in their hands as they went into that crowd?

CONNELLY: They had batons.

WEINGLASS: How were they holding their batons? Could you indicate that to the jury?

CONNELLY: When the wedge first started coming into the crowd, they were holding their batons, I believe, with both hands.

WEINGLASS: And did they begin to use their batons?

CONNELLY: Yes sir, I believe they did.

WEINGLASS: With one hand?

CONNELLY: Yes, sir.

WEINGLASS: In a swinging fashion?

CONNELLY: Yes, sir.

WEINGLASS: Striking the people in front of them?

CONNELLY: Yes, sir.

WEINGLASS: Did you see anybody go down under the force and impact of the batons?

CONNELLY: Of the wedge coming in, yes, people were falling down and running back.

WEINGLASS: Did you see anyone get hit on the head with a baton?

CONNELLY: I don't recall seeing anyone go down as a result of being struck with a baton.

WEINGLASS: Did you see anyone get hit on the head with a baton?

CONNELLY: No, I couldn't say that.

WEINGLASS: Did you see anyone get hit on the head with a baton?

CONNELLY: I saw clubs swung at people's heads, yes.

WEINGLASS: By the police?

wire on the front of them, is that correct?

ALBRIGHT: That is not correct, sir.

WEINGLASS: Tell us what you suggested to Rennie Davis.

ALBRIGHT: I suggested to Rennie Davis and some other people that a grappling hook be thrown into the barbed wire as it was being strung out from a truck.

WEINGLASS: From a truck?

ALBRIGHT: Yes, sir.

WEINGLASS: Is that from a military truck?

ALBRIGHT: I don't know, sir.

WEINGLASS: What kind of truck did you have in mind when you said it?

ALBRIGHT: Truck.

WEINGLASS: Any kind of truck? A moving van?

ALBRIGHT: Do you want an exact description of the truck, sir?

WEINGLASS: Yes, if you can give us the exact description of it, if you have it.

ALBRIGHT: Something like a two and a half ton military truck, with a canopy on the back of it.

WEINGLASS: You suggested that a grappling hook be used to somehow interfere with the wire mechanism of that truck? Is that correct?

ALBRIGHT: Yes, I did, sir.

WEINGLASS: People were asking for suggestions, but you were the only one to suggest that a military vehicle should be sabotaged, isn't that true?

ALBRIGHT: I think there were other suggestions, sir!

WEINGLASS: Now, I call your attention to Tuesday night, August 27th. You testified you attended a meeting in Grant Park. Is that correct?

ALBRIGHT: Yes, sir.

WEINGLASS: Was this one of the nights you were throwing rocks at the police yourself?

ALBRIGHT: I don't recall having thrown a rock on Tuesday night at the police.

WEINGLASS: Is it possible you might have thrown a can or stick, or some other object to provok the police?

ALBRIGHT: I might have thrown a can of paint later on that evening.

WEINGLASS: Do you recall being asked by the grand jury the following question: "Mr. Albright, do you recall having seen Jerry Rubin throwing an object at the police?"

SCHULTZ: If the Court please, what he should ask him: "Did you see Jerry Rubin throw an object at the police?" If he says "yes," then he can read this question and answer.

COURT: It seems to me, Mr., er, Weinglass, those are two different situations.

WEINGLASS: If Your Honor please, I spend a good deal of time with this witness . . .

COURT: I have spent a good deal of time listening to you also. Do you want a gold star for the time you spent?

KUNSTLER: Your Honor, I object to that, those insulting remarks to co-counsel.

COURT: I don't insult lawyers.

KUNSTLER: Sir, you just have, Your Honor.

COURT: Don't make a suggestion like that again, sir. If you will sit down, Mr. . . . .

KUNSTLER: Kunstler is the name, K—U—N—S—T—L—E—R.

COURT: I will let my ruling stand. Please continue Mr. . . . .

WEINGLASS: Weinglass, Your Honor. Did you, yourself, ever recall having seen Jerry Rubin throw an object at the police? Jerry Rubin?

ALBRIGHT: At the police themselves, *no*.

WEINGLASS: Thank you very much.

COURT: Is there any redirect examination?

SCHULTZ: Yes, Your Honor.

SEALE: Before the redirect, I would like to request again, demand, that I be able to cross-examine this witness. My lawyer is not here, I think I have a right to defend myself in this courtroom.

COURT: Let the record show the defendant Seale is again speaking in direct contempt of court.

SEALE: I would like to request that I be able to cross-examine the witness.

COURT: I deny your request, Mr. Seale.

SEALE: What about section 1982, title 42 of the code where it says the black man cannot be discriminated against in any legal defense in any court in America?

COURT: Mr. Seale do not attempt to indoctrinate me as to what the law says.

SEALE: You have George Washington and Thomas Jefferson standing in pictures behind you and they were slave owners. That's what they were. They owned slaves. You are acting in the same manner, denying me my constitutional rights of being able to cross-examine this witness. You have heard direct examination, we have cross-examination by the other defendants' lawyers, and I have a right to cross-examine the witness.

COURT: Mr. Seale, I have admonished you previously . . .

SEALE: I have a right to cross-examine this witness.

COURT: . . . what might happen to you if you keep on talking. Mr. Kunstler has his appearance on record here as your attorney.

SEALE: He is not. He is not. He is not my lawyer and you know that.

COURT: He is. I don't know . . .

SEALE: You know that.

COURT: I know that he is and I know that this is an entire device here . . .

SEALE: He is not my lawyer; you have forced—you have made your choice of who you think should represent me. That is not true. I made the choice of Charles R. Garry to represent me.

COURT: We are going to recess now, young man. If you keep this . . .

SEALE: Look, old man; if you keep denying me my constitutional rights . . .

SCHULTZ: May the record show, if the Court please, that while the marshals were restraining Bobby Seale, the defendant Dellinger physically attempted to interfere.

COURT: I am warning you, sir, that the law . . .

SEALE: Instead of warning, why don't you warn me that I have got a right to defend myself, huh?

COURT: I am warning you that the Court has a right to gag you. I don't want to do that. Under the law you may be gagged and chained to your chair.

SEALE: Gagged? I am being railroaded already.

COURT: And I might add, since it has been said here that all the defendants support you in your position, that I might conclude that they are bad risks for bail, and I say that to you, Mr. Kunstler, that if you can't control your client . . .

SEALE: I demand my right to be able to cross-examine this witness. He has made statements against me and I want my right to defend myself in this trial. I want my rights recognized.

COURT: Mr. Kunstler, I will address you if you stand up.

KUNSTLER: I was going to address you, Your Honor, because you made some remarks . . .

SEALE: He doesn't represent me. You can address him all you want. He doesn't represent me. He doesn't represent me.

KUNSTLER: Your Honor, you made a threat about my clients' bail.

COURT: I tell you that Mr. Dellinger—if that is his name . . .

DELLINGER: Yes, that is his name.

COURT: . . . has said here that they support the performances of this man, the statements of this man.

KUNSTLER: They support his right to have a lawyer or to defend himself. ·

COURT: You told me you were his lawyer.

KUNSTLER: Your Honor . . .

SEALE: He is not my lawyer.

KUNSTLER: Your Honor, we have gone over that.

SEALE: I told you I fired him before the trial began.

COURT: You haven't explained . . .

KUNSTLER: I told you on the 27th and I told you on the 30th.

COURT: I tell you, someday you will have to explain it.

KUNSTLER: That is another threat to the lawyers, Your Honor. We have had so many that . . .

COURT: Now I will tell you this, that since it has been said here that all of these defendants support this man in what he is doing, I over the noon hour will reflect on whether they are good risks for bail and I shall give serious consideration to the termination of their bail if you can't control your clients.

SEALE: I am not—I am not a defendant, he is not my lawyer. I want my right to defend myself.

KUNSTLER: Your Honor, they said this morning they fully supported his right to defend himself or have a lawyer of his choice, and if that is the price of their bail, then I guess that will have to be the price of their bail.

COURT: Let me tell you . . .

SEALE: I have the right to defend myself. That's what you . . .

COURT: Will Mr. Marshal have that man sit down.

MARSHAL: Mr. Seale, sit down.

SEALE: You are trying to make jive bargaining operations and that's different from the right I have. I have a right to speak out on behalf of my defense and you know it. You know it. Why don't you recognize my right to defend myself?

COURT: Mr. Seale . . .

SEALE: I request again—demand, to cross-examine the witness.

COURT: I will issue the orders around here.

SEALE: I don't take orders from racist judges. We protested our rights for 400 years and we have been shot and killed and murdered, brutalized and oppressed for 400 years.

COURT: Did you get that outburst, Miss Reporter?

REPORTER: Yes, sir.

COURT: If you continue with that sort of thing, you may expect to be punished. I warned you right through this trial and I warn you again, sir.

SEALE: Why don't you knock me on the mouth? Try that. You represent the corruptness of this rotten, fascist government for 400 years.

COURT: I will tell you what I indicated yesterday might happen to you . . .

SEALE: Happen to me? What can happen to me more than what Thomas Jefferson and George Washington did to black people in slavery?

COURT: Have him sit down, Mr. Marshal. Well, I have been called a racist, a fascist. He has pointed to the picture of George Washington and called him a slave owner and . . .

SEALE: They were slave owners. Look at history.

COURT: As though I had anything to do with that.

KUNSTLER: We all share a common guilt, Your Honor.

SEALE: You have done everything you could with those jive lying witnesses up there presented by these pig agents of the Government to lie and condone some rotten fascist, racist crap by racist cops and pigs that beat people's heads . . .

COURT: Mr. Seale, do you want to stop or do you want me to direct the marshal . . .

SEALE: . . . and I demand my constitutional rights—demand, demand, demand!

COURT: Take the defendant into the room and deal with him as he shouled be dealt with in this circumstance. We will take a recess.

Blackout.

SCENE TEN

FORAN: Your Honor, if Mr. Seale would express to the Court his willingness to be quiet, would the Court entertain the possibility of Mr. Seale being unbound and ungagged?

COURT: I have tried with all my heart to get him to sit in this Court and be tried fairly, and I have been greeted on every occasion with all sort of vicious invective. Mr. Seale, all of your Constitutional and statutory rights have been and will be preserved in this trial. I want you to conduct yourself in a manner that is gentlemanly. I ask you, therefore, and you may indicate by raising your head up and down or shaking your head, side to side, meaning no, whether or not I have your assurance that you will not disrupt this trial if you are permitted to resume your former place. Will you, sir?

SEALE: (*Gagged.*) I can't speak.

COURT: I can't understand you.

SEALE: (*Gagged.*) I want to defend myself.

COURT: Mr. Marshal. (*Gag tightened.*) Well, Mr. Foran, I tried to do what you suggested.

FORAN: Your Honor. I would also like the record to show that just prior to Mr. Seale speaking through his gag, the defendant Davis was whispering to him. Encouraging him.

COURT: Mr. Seale, I order you to refrain from making those noises. Now Mr. Foran do you have any redirect examination of this witness?

KUNSTLER: Your Honor, before Mr. Foran proceeds, I just want to move for the removal of the irons and the gag on the ground that Mr. Seale was attempting to assert his right to self-defense under the Constitution.

COURT: These measures have been taken to ensure the proper conduct of this trial which I am obligated to do under the law. The motion of Mr. Kunstler will be denied.

Blackout.

SCENE ELEVEN

Testimony of Government Witness RICHARD GRANDHOLM, *a Chicago police officer*

COURT: Will you continue with your cross-examination?

WEINGLASS: If Your Honor please, just before that I would like to inform the Court that standing here as I am just five feet from a man who is shackled and bound and gagged and who, when the jury is not in this courtroom . . .

COURT: Will you continue with your cross-examination?

WEINGLASS: . . . is physically assaulted by the marshals . . .

COURT: If you have any observation about any other thing, I will permit you to make it at the end of your cross-examination.

WEINGLASS: I am attempting to . . .

COURT: Please continue with your cross-examination of this witness.

WEINGLASS: After you heard Mr. Froines make that speech, did you make any arrests?

GRANDHOLM: No, sir.

WEINGLASS: Now you did see what you described as a couple making love in a tree, did you not?

GRANDHOLM: I did.

WEINGLASS: You saw them having intercourse in a tree, isn't that correct?

GRANDHOLM: Yes, sir.

WEINGLASS: And that was what kind of tree, do you remember?

GRANDHOLM: I don't know what kind of tree it was, sir.

WEINGLASS: You're quite sure you hadn't wandered into the zoo.

GRANDHOLM: Quite sure.

WEINGLASS: Did you arrest those people?

GRANDHOLM: No, sir.

WEINGLASS: In fact you went right under the tree and you looked up, isn't that correct?

GRANDHOLM: No, sir, I was under . . .

WEINGLASS: You weren't under the tree looking up?

GRANDHOLM: I was under the tree. I didn't walk under. I was under there at the time.

WEINGLASS: And then suddenly your attention was drawn to the fact that someone was making love over your head, isn't that correct?

GRANDHOLM: That is right.

WEINGLASS: And you looked up?

GRANDHOLM: I did.

WEINGLASS: How long did you look?

GRANDHOLM: Two seconds.

WEINGLASS: And then you walked on about your business, is that correct.

GRANDHOLM: Yes, sir.

WEINGLASS: Were you concerned about their safety?

GRANDHOLM: No, sir.

KUNSTLER: If Your Honor please, the cuff holding Mr. Seale's hand is digging into his hand, and he appears to be trying to free his hand from that pressure. Could he be assisted?

COURT: If the marshal has concluded that he needs assistance, of course.

MARSHAL: No, Your Honor.

COURT: Please continue with your cross-examination, Mr. Weinstein.

WEINGLASS: Weinglass, Your Honor. If Your Honor please, Mr. Seale is having difficulty. He is in extreme discomfort.

COURT: He is being treated in accordance with the law.

KUNSTLER: Not the Constitution of the United States, Your Honor, which is the supreme law. He has the right to defend himself.

COURT: I don't need someone to come here from New York or wherever it is you come from to tell me that there is a Constitution in the United States.

KUNSTLER: I feel someone needs to tell someone, Your Honor. It is not being observed in this Court, if that is the treatment a man gets for defending himself.

COURT: Read the books. You read the books and you will find that the Court has the authority to do what is being done and I will not let this trial be broken up by his conduct.

KUNSTLER: Your Honor, we feel that it is impossible for white men to sit in this room while a black man is in chains and continue . . .

COURT: I wish you wouldn't talk about the distinction between white and black in this courtroom.

KUNSTLER: A lot of the seven white men . . .

COURT: I have lived a long time and you are the first person who has ever suggested that I have discriminated against a black man. Come into my chambers and I will show you on the wall what one of the great newspapers of this city said about me in respect to the school segregation case.

KUNSTLER: Your Honor, this is not a time for self-praise on either side of the lectern.

COURT: It isn't self-praise, sir. It is defense. I won't have a lawyer stand before the bar and accuse me of being a bigot.

KUNSTLER: For God's sakes, Your Honor, we are seeking a solution of a human problem here, not whether you feel good or bad.

COURT: Don't shout at me. I don't like that. (*To* WEINGLASS.) Mr. . . .

WEINGLASS: It is impossible for me at this point to proceed with the cross-examination of this witness, while one man is here receiving the treatment that Mr. Seale is being dealt at your hand.

COURT: If it isn't possible, then you may sit down. Do you want to continue with your examination?

WEINGLASS: I do not.

COURT: Then you may sit down.

SCHULTZ: Your Honor, I think we are, of course, concerned. He looks very uncomfortable.

KUNSTLER: Your Honor, are we going to stop this medieval torture that is going on in this courtroom? I think this is a disgrace.

SEALE: The motherfucker is tight and it is stopping my blood.

COURT: Listen to him now.

KUNSTLER: Your Honor, we cannot hear him because of the binding and gag on him.

COURT: Why should I have to go through a trial and be assailed in an obscene manner?

DAVIS: Ladies and gentlemen of the jury, he was being tortured while you were out of this room by these marshals. It is terrible what is happening.

COURT: Will you ask that man to sit down, Mr. Marshal?

FORAN: That is Mr. Davis, Your Honor.

HAYDEN: Your Honor, could I address you?

COURT: No, you may not, sir. You have a lawyer; that is what lawyers are for.

HAYDEN: All I want to say is that . . .

COURT: Sit down, please.

HAYDEN: Bobby Seale should not be put in a position of slavery.

COURT: Mr. Marshal, tell that man to sit down. What is his name?

HAYDEN: My name is Tom Hayden, Your Honor. I would just like to . . .

COURT: Let the record show that Mr. Tom Hayden persisted in speaking despite the Court's direction that he sit down. Who is that man who is talking?

FROINES: Your Honor, he is being choked to death, tortured . . .

SEALE: The judge is not—he is not trying to give you no fair trial.

COURT: Mr. Marshal . . . (*The* MARSHALS *remove* SEALE.)

HOFFMAN: You may as well kill him if you are going to gag him.

FORAN: That was the defendant Hoffman who spoke.

COURT: You are not permitted to address the Court, Mr. Hoffman. You have a lawyer.

HOFFMAN: This isn't a court. This is an inquisition!

KUNSTLER: Can we have somebody with Mr. Seale? We don't trust those marshals.

COURT: The marshals will take care of him.

RUBIN: Take care of him?

HAYDEN: Yeah, they're taking care of him right now by beating him!

COURT: Let that appear on the record, Miss Reporter.

Blackout.

PHOTO COURTESY THE ODYSSEY THEATRE

SCENE TWELVE

November 3, 1969.

COURT: I find that the acts, statements and conduct of the defendant Bobby Seale constitute a deliberate and willful attack upon the administration of justice, and attempt to sabotage the functioning of the federal judiciary system and misconduct of so grave a character as to make the mere imposition of a fine a futile gesture and a wholly insignificant punishment.

Accordingly, I adjudge Bobby G. Seale guilty of each and every contempt specification referred to in my oral observations of direct contempt of Court. The defendant Seale will be committed to the custody of the Attorney General of the United States for imprisonment for a term of three months on each and every specification, the sentences to run consecutively. (*To* DEFENDANTS.) Quiet! Mr. Seale, you have the right to speak now. I will hear you.

SEALE: For myself?

COURT: In your own behalf, yes.

SEALE: How come I couldn't speak before?

COURT: This is a special occasion.

SEALE: Wait a minute. Now are you going to try—you punish me for attempting to speak for myself before? Now after you punish me, you sit up there and say something about you can speak? What kind of jive is that? I don't understand it. What kind of court is this? Is this a court? It must be some kind of fascist operation like I see in my mind, you know—I don't understand you.

COURT: I am calling on you . . .

SEALE: What am I supposed to speak about? I still haven't got the right to defend myself. I would like to speak about that. I would like to—since you let me stand up and speak, can I speak about— can I defend myself?

COURT: I have tried to make it clear.

SEALE: All you can make clear to me is that you don't want me. You don't want to listen to me. If a black man stands up and speaks, if a black man demands his rights, if a black requests and argues his rights, what do you do? You're talking about punishing.

COURT: I direct the United States Attorney to prepare from the oral remarks I made here a certificate of contempt for my signature, together with a judgment and commitment order. How soon, Miss Reporter, before it is written? I am glad I have got both of you here.

REPORTER: Six o'clock, Your Honor.

COURT: Get it to Mr. Foran as soon as you can and the case will be continued until tomorrow morning. There will be an order declaring a mistrial as to the defendant Bobby G. Seale, and not as to any other defendants.

SEALE: What's the cat trying to pull now? I'm leaving the—I can't stay?

SCHULTZ: Will Your Honor set a trial date for the defendant Seale?

COURT: Yes. Yes.

SEALE: I demand an immediate trial right now.

COURT: Yes, we will give you a trial date.

SEALE: I'm talking about now. I don't want to be taken out. I have a right to go through with this trial.

COURT: A mistrial has been declared with respect to you, sir. Your trial will be conducted on April 23, 1970, at ten o'clock in the morning.

SEALE: I want it immediate, right now, though.

COURT: I'm sorry, I can't try two cases at one time, sir.

SEALE: I still want an immediate trial. You can't call it a mistrial. I'm put in jail for four months for nothing? I want...

COURT: All right, Mr. Marshal...

KUNSTLER: Your Honor...

SEALE: I want...

COURT: Mr. Marshal.

KUNSTLER: The right of a black man to defend himself...

COURT: I will not hear you any longer.

FORAN: No man, black, white, green, or polka-dotted has any right to disrupt a Court of the United States.

SEALE: I'm not disrupting...

HAYDEN: Now they are going to beat him!

DELLINGER: Somebody go to protect him!

FORAN: Your Honor, may the record show that that is Mr. Dellinger saying someone go to protect him...

RUBIN: May the record show that Foran is a Nazi.

FORAN: And the other comment is by Mr. Rubin.

SCHULTZ: And after that it was Mr. Hayden, Your Honor.

HAYDEN: I was trying to protect Mr. Seale, Your Honor. A man is supposed to be quiet when he sees another's nose being smashed?!

KUNSTLER: This is not a court, Your Honor. It's a medieval torture chamber.

FORAN: That man goes on and on.

COURT: Everything you say will be taken down.

SEALE: You fascist dogs.

KUNSTLER: Your Honor, this is a disgrace. We would like the names of these marshals . . .

COURT: Don't point at me in that manner.

KUNSTLER: Your Honor, this is an unholy disgrace to the law.

FORAN: Created by Mr. Kunstler.

KUNSTLER: Created by nothing other than what you have done to this man.

SEALE: You low-life son-of-a-bitch. (MARSHAL *strikes* SEALE. RUBIN *leaps over table.*)

COURT: Did you get that Miss Reporter?

KUNSTLER: They are assaulting the other defendants as well!

HOFFMAN: You come down here and watch it, judge. It's the same thing that happened last year in Chicago, the exact same thing.

COURT: Take that down. The Court will be in recess.

Blackout.

A C T   T W O

S C E N E   O N E

Vietnam Moratorium Day. October 15, 1969.
Case for the Defense.

CLERK: Will all please rise. (JUDGE *enters.*) United States District Court for the Northern District of Illinois is now in session. The Honorable Julius J. Hoffman presiding. Please be seated. (*The names of the war dead are read by the* DEFENDANTS.)

DELLINGER: Mr. Hoffman, we are observing the Vietnam moratorium.

COURT: I am Judge Hoffman, sir.

DELLINGER: I believe in equality, sir, so I prefer to call people Mr. or by their first name.

COURT: Sit down. The clerk is about to call the case.

DELLINGER: I want to explain to you we are reading the names of the war dead.

MARSHAL: Sit down, Mr. Dellinger.

DELLINGER: We were reading the names of the dead from both sides.

MARSHAL: Sit down.

DELLINGER: All right. I'll sit down.

CLERK: No. 69 CR 180. United States of America vs. David T. Dellinger, et al. Case on trial.

KUNSTLER: Your Honor, the defendants who were not permitted to be absent today or to have a court recess for the Vietnam moratorium brought in an American flag and an NLF flag which they placed on the counsel table to commemorate the dead Americans and the dead Vietnamese in this long and brutal war.

COURT: We have an American flag in the corner. Haven't you seen it during the three and a half months you have been here?

KUNSTLER: Yes, but we wanted the juxtaposition of the two flags together in one place.

COURT: I point out, standing in the courtroom—and it has been here since this building was opened—is an American flag.

HOFFMAN: We don't consider this table a part of the courtroom and we want to furnish it in our own way.

MARSHAL: Sit down.

COURT: To place the flag of an enemy country.

KUNSTLER: No, Your Honor. There is no declared war.

HAYDEN: Are you at war with Vietnam?

COURT: Any country—let that appear on the record. I will ask you to sit down.

KUNSTLER: Your Honor . . .

FORAN: Your Honor, this is outrageous. This man is a mouthpiece. Look at him, wearing an armband like his clients.

COURT: Note has been duly made on the record.

KUNSTLER: Your Honor, I just want to object to Mr. Foran yelling in the presence of the jury . . .

FORAN: Oh, Your Honor . . .

KUNSTLER: Your Honor, I think that the expression on Mr. Foran's face speaks louder than any picture can tell . . .

FORAN: Of my contempt for Mr. Kunstler, Your Honor.

KUNSTLER: I am wearing an armband in memoriam to the dead, Your Honor, which is no disgrace in this country. I want him admonished, Your Honor.

COURT: Did you say you want to admonish me?

KUNSTLER: No. I want you to admonish him.

COURT: Let the record show I do not admonish the United States Attorney because he was properly representing his client, the United States of America.

DELLINGER: We would like to propose . . .

SCHULTZ: If the Court please . . .

FORAN: If the Court please, Your Honor, may the marshal take that man into custody.

DELLINGER: A moment of silence . . .

SCHULTZ: Your Honor, this man . . .

DELLINGER: We only want a moment of silence . . .

SCHULTZ: Your Honor, this man said on the elevator on the way up here . . .

DELLINGER: We only want a moment of silence.

FORAN: Your Honor, I object to this man speaking out in court.

COURT: You needn't object. I forbid him to disrupt the Court. I note for the record that his name is . . .

DELLINGER: David Dellinger is my name.

COURT: You needn't interrupt my sentence for me.

DELLINGER: You have been interrupting ours.

COURT: The name of this man who has attempted to disrupt the proceedings is David Dellinger and the record will clearly indicate that, Miss Reporter.

Blackout.

SCENE TWO

Testimony of Defendant RENNIE DAVIS

FORAN: Objection.

COURT: Sustained.

WEINGLASS: Could you relate now to the Court and jury the words you spoke, as best as you can recall, on that particular night?

DAVIS: I began by holding up a small steel ball about the size of a tennis ball and I said, "This bomb was dropped on a city of 100,000 people, a city called Nam Ding, by an American fighter jet," about 640 of these steel balls were spewed into the sky from one large bomb. And I said, "When this ball strikes a building or the ground an explosion occurs which sends out about 300 steel pellets. With 640 of these bombs going off, you can throw steel pellets over an area about a thousand yards long and about 250 yards wide, and every living thing exposed in that 1,000-yard area will die." I said, "This bomb would not destroy this building, it would not damage the walls, the ceiling, the floor." I said, "If it is dropped on a city, it takes life but leaves the institutions. It is the ideal weapon, you see, for the mentality who reasons that life is less precious than property."

I said that in 1967, "One out of every two bombs dropped on North Vietnam by the American government was this weapon. And in 1967 the American government told the American public that in North Vietnam it was hitting only military targets. Yet what I saw was pagodas that had been gutted, schoolhouses that had been razed, population centers that had been leveled."

WEINGLASS: If the Court please, the Defense would like to offer into evidence D-235, the anti-personnel bomb...

FORAN: Your Honor, the Government objects to this exhibit. The Vietnamese war has nothing whatsoever to do with the charges in this indictment.

COURT: I sustain the objection of the Government. Mr. Marshal, will you remove that man sitting there. Ask him to leave. He was laughing right at me while I was speaking.

WEINGLASS: I was standing right here. Mr. Albert did not laugh.

COURT: Mr. Albert was laughing right at me.

HAYDEN: Your Honor...

COURT: I ask Mr. Albert to leave.

HOFFMAN: I was laughing.

HAYDEN: It was me that was laughing, Your Honor.

COURT: I can't order you to leave. You are at trial. Mr. Marshal, take Mr. Albert out.

DELLINGER: This is an injustice.

KUNSTLER: That is a lawyer who is part of our defense team.

COURT: He is not a lawyer permitted to practice in this Court.

KUNSTLER: You are removing a lawyer from the defense table.

COURT: No, he is not a lawyer permitted to practice here.

KUNSTLER: That doesn't matter, Your Honor, he is...

DELLINGER: He wasn't laughing.

KUNSTLER: You have given him permission to sit here.

COURT: I withdraw the permission.

KUNSTLER: You are depriving us of a lawyer at our Defense table.

COURT: That is just too bad. You will have to suffer through without him.

KUNSTLER: He is a member of the bar of the District of Columbia. He had been assisting us for three months through this trial.

COURT: Let him go back to the District of Columbia. I will not have him here while I am trying to rule.

KUNSTLER: But he didn't laugh, Your Honor. If he laughed that is one thing, perhaps, but two defendants have admitted laughing.

COURT: No, Mr. Albert will not be readmitted. He is not permitted to practice here, and for good and sufficient reason I order him out.

KUNSTLER: Put him in the stand and ask him whether he laughed.

COURT: Will you sit down please.

KUNSTLER: He wouldn't lie under oath.

COURT: Will you sit down.

KUNSTLER: I guess I have no alternative, Your Honor.

COURT: That is right.

Blackout.

SCENE THREE

Testimony of Defendant ABBOTT H. HOFFMAN

WEINGLASS: Will you please identify yourself for the record?

HOFFMAN: My name is Abbie. I am an orphan of America.

WEINGLASS: Where do you reside?

HOFFMAN: I live in Woodstock Nation.

WEINGLASS: Will you tell the Court and jury where that is?

HOFFMAN: Yes. It is a nation of alienated young people. We carry it around with us in the same way the Sioux Indians carried the Sioux Nation around with them. It is a nation dedicated to co-operation versus competition, to the idea that people should have a better means of exchange than property or money, that there should be some other basis for human interaction. It is a nation dedicated to . . .

COURT: Excuse me, sir. Read the question to the witness, please.

REPORTER: "Will you tell the Court and jury where it is?"

COURT: Just where it is, that's all.

HOFFMAN: It is in my mind and in the minds of my brothers and sisters. It does not consist of property or material, but rather of ideas and certain values; those values being co-operation versus competition, and . . .

SCHULTZ: That doesn't say where Woodstock Nation, whatever that is, is.

WEINGLASS: Your Honor, the witness has identified it as being a state of mind and he has, I think, a right to define that state of mind.

HOFFMAN: This is going to be a very exciting cross-examination.

COURT: No, we want the place of residence, if he has one, place of doing business, if you have a business, or both if you desire to tell both. One address will be sufficient. But, nothing about philosophy or India, sir. Just where you live if you have a place to live. Now you said Woodstock. In what state is Woodstock?

HOFFMAN: It is the state of mind, in the mind of myself and my brothers and sisters. It's a conspiracy.

WEINGLASS: Abbie, could you tell the Court and jury...

SCHULTZ: His name isn't Abbie. I object to this informality.

COURT: Objection sustained. Yes, use his full name, Mr. Winegrass.

HOFFMAN: Winegrass, it's my favorite combination!

WEINGLASS: Can you tell the Court and jury your present age?

HOFFMAN: My age is 33. I am a child of the 60s.

WEINGLASS: When were you born?

HOFFMAN: Psychologically, 1960.

SCHULTZ: Objection.

COURT: I sustain the objection.

WEINGLASS: Between the date of your birth and May 1, 1960, what if anything occurred in your life?

HOFFMAN: Nothing. I believe it's called an American education.

SCHULTZ: Objection.

COURT: I sustain the objection.

HOFFMAN: Huh?

WEINGLASS: Can you tell the Court and jury what is your present occupation?

HOFFMAN: I am a cultural revolutionary. Well, I am really a defendant—full time.

WEINGLASS: Abbie Hoffman, prior to coming to Chicago, did you enter into an agreement with David Dellinger, John Froines, Tom Hayden, Jerry Rubin, Lee Weiner or Rennie Davis, to come to the city of Chicago for the purpose of encouraging and promoting violence during the convention week?

HOFFMAN: An agreement?

WEINGLASS: Yes.

HOFFMAN: We couldn't agree on lunch.

*   *   *

SCHULTZ: It was in December of 1967 that you and Rubin and Paul Krassner created the Yippie myth, is that right?

HOFFMAN: And Nancy Kurshan and Anita Hoffman—that's the woman I live with. It's not just men that participate in myths.

SCHULTZ: And the myth was created in order to get people to come to Chicago, isn't that right, Mr. Hoffman?

HOFFMAN: That's right, Mr. Schultz—that was one reason, to create—the other was to put forth a certain concept, a certain life style.

SCHULTZ: And part of your myth was "We'll burn Chicago to the ground," isn't that right?

HOFFMAN: It was part of the myth that there were trainloads of dynamite headed for Chicago; it was part of the myth that they were going to form white vigilante groups and round up demonstrators. All these things were part of the myth. A myth is a process of telling stories, most of which aren't true.

SCHULTZ: On the 7th of August, you told David Stahl you were going to have nude-ins in the parks of Chicago, didn't you?

HOFFMAN: A nude-in? I don't believe I would use that phrase, no. Quite frankly, I don't think it's very poetic.

SCHULTZ: You told him, did you not, Mr. Hoffman, that you would have . . .

HOFFMAN: I'm not even sure I know what it is, a nude-in.

SCHULTZ: Public fornication.

KUNSTLER: I object to this because Mr. Schultz is acting like a dirty old man.

SCHULTZ: No, we aren't getting into dirty old men here.

COURT: Objection denied.

HOFFMAN: I don't mind talking about it.

SCHULTZ: Mr. Hoffman—Your Honor, Mr. Davis is having a very fine time here whispering at me. He has been doing it for the last twenty minutes. I would ask Mr. Davis to stop distracting me.

COURT: Try not to speak too loudly, Mr. Davis.

DAVIS: Yes, sir.

COURT: Go ahead.

HOFFMAN: Go ahead, Dick.

SCHULTZ: "And there will be acid for all," that was another one of your Yippie myths, isn't that right?

HOFFMAN: That was well known.

SCHULTZ: Was there any acid in Lincoln Park in Chicago?

HOFFMAN: In the reservoir, in the lake?

SCHULTZ: No, among the people.

HOFFMAN: Among the people was there LSD? Well, there might have been. I don't know. It's colorless, odorless and tasteless. One can never tell.

SCHULTZ: What about the honey. Was there anything special about any honey in Lincoln Park?

HOFFMAN: There was honey, there was—I was told there was honey—I was getting stoned eating brownies. Honey, yes. Lots of people were . . .

SCHULTZ: Was there LSD to your knowledge in both the honey and in some brownies? Is that right?

HOFFMAN: I would have to be a chemist to know that for a fact. It is colorless, odorless and tasteless.

SCHULTZ: Didn't you state on a prior occasion that Ed Sanders passed out from too much honey?

HOFFMAN: Yes. People passed out.

COURT: You have answered the question.

HOFFMAN: Yes. Passed out from honey? Sure. Is that illegal?

SCHULTZ: And a man named Spade passed out on honey.

HOFFMAN: Yes. I made up that name. Frankie Spade, wasn't it? It must have been strong honey.

COURT: The last observation of the witness may go out and the witness is directed again not to make any gratuitous observations.

HOFFMAN: Where do they go when they go out?

COURT: Will you remain quiet while I am making a ruling? I know you have no respect for me.

KUNSTLER: Your Honor, that is totally unwarranted.

COURT: I don't need any argument on that one. The witness turned his back on me while he was on the witness stand.

HOFFMAN: I was just looking at the pictures of the longhairs up on the wall.

COURT: And I don't like being laughed at by a witness in this Court, sir.

HOFFMAN: I know that laughing is a crime. I already . . .

COURT: I direct you not to laugh at an observation by the Court. I don't laugh at you.

HOFFMAN: Are you sure?

COURT: I haven't laughed at you during all of the many weeks and months of this trial. Mr. Schultz, ask your next question, please?

SCHULTZ: Mr. Hoffman, isn't it a fact that one of the reasons why you came to Chicago was simply to wreck American society?

HOFFMAN: My feeling at the time, and still is, that this society is going to wreck itself. Our role is to survive. Could I have some more water, Judge?

COURT: Give him some water please.

HOFFMAN: This trial is bad for my health.

*   *   *

WEINGLASS: Now in exorcising the Pentagon, were there any plans to raise the building off the ground?

HOFFMAN: Yes. When we were arrested they asked us what we were doing. We said it was to measure the Pentagon and we wanted a permit to raise it 300 feet in the air, and they said, "How about ten?" So we said, "OK." And they threw us out of the Pentagon and we went back to New York and had a press conference and told them what it was about.

We also introduced a drug called "lace," which, when you squirted it at policemen it made them take their clothes off and make love, a very potent drug.

SCHULTZ: I would ask Mr. Weinglass please to get on with the trial of this case and stop playing around with raising the Pentagon ten or 300 feet off the ground.

KUNSTLER: Your Honor, this is not playing around. This is a deadly serious business. The whole issue in this case is language, what is meant by saying...

SCHULTZ: This is not—this is totally irrelevant.

COURT: Let Mr. Weinglass defend himself.

WEINGLASS: Your Honor, I am glad to see that Mr. Schultz finally concedes that things like levitating the Pentagon building, putting LSD in the water, nominating a pig for president are all playing around. I am willing to concede that fact, that it was all playing around; it was a play idea of the witness, and if he is willing to concede it we can all go home. Because Mr. Schultz is treating all these things as deadly serious.

*   *   *

SCHULTZ: Did you see some people urinate on the Pentagon?

HOFFMAN: On the Pentagon itself?

SCHULTZ: Or at the Pentagon?

HOFFMAN: In that general area of Washington?

SCHULTZ: Yes.

HOFFMAN: There were in all over 100,000 people. That is, people have that biological habit.

SCHULTZ: And did you?

HOFFMAN: Yes.

SCHULTZ: Did you symbolically?

HOFFMAN: Did I go and look?

SCHULTZ: Did you—did you symbolically urinate on the Pentagon, Mr. Hoffman?

HOFFMAN: I symbolically urinate on the Pentagon?

SCHULTZ: Yes.

HOFFMAN: Nearby, yes, in the bushes there, maybe 3,000 feet away from the Pentagon. I didn't get that close. Pee on the walls of the Pentagon? You're getting to be out of sight, actually. Do you think there is a law against it?

SCHULTZ: Are you done, Mr. Hoffman?

HOFFMAN: I am done when you are.

SCHULTZ: Did you ever on a prior occasion state that a sense of integration possesses you and comes from pissing on the Pentagon?

HOFFMAN: What I said was that from combining political attitudes with biological necessity, there is a sense of integration, yes. I think I said it that way, not the way you said it.

SCHULTZ: You had a good time at the Pentagon, didn't you, Mr. Hoffman?

HOFFMAN: Yes, I did. I am having a good time now. In fact, I'm starting to feel that biological necessity right now. Could I be excused for a brief recess.

COURT: We will take a brief recess, ladies and gentlemen of the jury.

HOFFMAN: Just a brief . . .

COURT: We will take a brief recess with my usual orders. A very brief recess.

Blackout.

SCENE FOUR

Testimony of Defense Witness ALLEN GINSBERG

WEINGLASS: Mr. Ginsberg, calling your attention to the month of February, 1968, did you have any occasion in that month to meet with Abbie Hoffman?

GINSBERG: Yeah.

WEINGLASS: Do you recall what Mr. Hoffman said in the course of that meeting?

GINSBERG: Yippee! Among other things. He said that politics had become theatre and magic; that it was the manipulation of imagery through the mass media that was confusing and hypnotizing the people in the United States and making them accept a war which they did not really believe in; that people were involved in a life style that was intolerable to younger folk, which involved brutality and police violence as well as the larger violence in Vietnam. And that ourselves might be able to get together in

Chicago and invite teachers to present different ideas about what is wrong with the planet, what we can do to solve the pollution crisis, what we can do to solve the Vietnam War. To present different ideas to make society more sacred, less commercial, less materialistic, what we could do to uplevel or improve the whole tone of the trap we all felt ourselves in as the population grew and as politics became more and more violent and chaotic.

WEINGLASS: After he spoke to you, what if any was your response to his suggestions?

GINSBERG: I was worried as to whether or not the whole scene would get violent. I was worried whether, you know, the government would let us do something that was funnier, or prettier or more charming than what was going to be going on in the Convention Hall.

FORAN: I ask that statement be stricken; it was not responsive.

COURT: I sustain the objection.

GINSBERG: Sir, that was our conversation.

COURT: I direct the jury to disregard the last answer of the witness.

WEINGLASS: Your Honor, I would like to be informed by the Court how that answer was not responsive to that question. It seemed to me directly responsive.

FORAN: Your Honor, he asked him what he said and he answered by saying what he was wondering.

GINSBERG: Oh, I am sorry then. I said to Abbie that I was worried about violence.

COURT: I have ruled on the objection. Ask another question if you like.

WEINGLASS: Did you hear Jerry Rubin make a speech in Lincoln Park on August 24th?

GINSBERG: Yes. Jerry Rubin said that he didn't think that it would be a good thing to fight with the police over that eleven o'clock curfew.

WEINGLASS: At approximately ten-thirty that evening what was happening in the park?

GINSBERG: There were several thousand young people gathered, waiting. It was dark, there were some bonfires burning in trash cans. Everybody was standing around not knowing what to do. Then, there was a sudden burst of light in the center of the park and a group of policemen moved in fast and kicked over the bonfires.

WEINGLASS: What did you do when you observed the police doing this?

GINSBERG: I started the chant Ommmmm.

DEFENDANTS: Ommmmm.

FORAN: All right, we have had a demonstration.

COURT: All right.

FORAN: From here on I object.

COURT: You haven't said you objected.

FORAN: I do after the second one.

COURT: After two of them? I sustain the objection.

FORAN: I have no objection to the two Oms we have had. However, I just didn't want to go on all morning.

COURT: Mr. Feinglass will you please continue with the questioning of this witness?

KUNSTLER: Your Honor, so the record may be clear. I don't think Mr. Weinglass noticed the Feinglass.

COURT: Oh, I did myself. I inserted an *F* there instead of the *W* you deserve, Mr. Weinglass. Mr. Weinglass. Somebody held up the name.

KUNSTLER: We have the name here, Your Honor.

COURT: Yes.

HOFFMAN: Here it is. Shall we put it on him?

COURT: Yes, yes. Please continue . . .

WEINGLASS: Now Mr. Ginsberg, where if anywhere did you go on Tuesday night, August 27?

GINSBERG: The group I was with, Jean Genet, William Burroughs and Terry Southern, all went back to Lincoln Park.

WEINGLASS: What was occurring in the park as you got there?

GINSBERG: There was a great crowd lining the outskirts of the park and at the center of the park there was a group of ministers and rabbis who had elevated a great cross about ten feet high in the middle of a circle of people who were sitting around quietly, listening to the ministers conduct a ceremony.

WEINGLASS: After the ceremony was over, what if anything occurred?

GINSBERG: The ministers lifted up the cross and took it to the edge of the crowd and set it down facing the lights where the police were. In other words they confronted the police lines with the cross of Christ.

WEINGLASS: After the ministers moved the cross to the other location which you have just indicated, what happened?

GINSBERG: After, I don't know, a short period of time, there was a burst of smoke and teargas round the cross and the cross was enveloped in teargas and the people who were carrying the cross were enveloped in teargas which slowly began drifting over the crowd.

WEINGLASS: And when you saw the persons with the cross and the cross being gassed, what if anything did you do?

GINSBERG: I turned to Burroughs and said, "They have gassed the cross of Christ."

FORAN: Objection if the Court please. I ask the answer be stricken.

COURT: I sustain the objection.

WEINGLASS: Without relating what you said, Mr. Ginsberg, what did you do at that time?

GINSBERG: I took Bill Burroughs' hand and took Terry Southern's hand and we turned from the cross which was covered with gas in the glary lights that were coming from the police lights that were shining through the teargas on the cross and walked slowly out of the park.

WEINGLASS: Thank you. Nothing further.

COURT: You may cross-examine. Mr. Foran.

FORAN: Mr. Ginsberg, you've been named a sort of religious leader of the Yippies and you testified concerning a number of books of poetry that you have written?

GINSBERG: Yes.

FORAN: In *The Empty Mirror,* there is a poem called "The Night Apple"?

GINSBERG: Yes.

FORAN: Would you recite that for the jury?

GINSBERG: "The Night Apple."

> Last night I dreamed
> of one I loved
> for seven long years,
> but I saw no face,
> only the familiar
> presence of the body;
> sweat skin eyes
> feces urine sperm
> saliva all one
> odor and mortal taste.

FORAN: Could you explain to the jury having said that, what the religious significance of that poem is?

GINSBERG: I could, if you would take a wet dream as a religious experience. It is a description of a wet dream, sir.

FORAN: Now, Mr. Ginsberg, you testified when you met Abbie Hoffman in Lincoln Park, you said when you met him you kissed him?

GINSBERG: Yes.

FORAN: Is he an intimate friend of yours?

GINSBERG: I felt very intimate with him. I saw he was struggling to manifest a beautiful thing, and I felt very good towards him.

FORAN: And do you consider him an intimate friend of yours?

GINSBERG: I don't see him that often, but I do see him often enough and have worked with him often enough to feel intimate with him, yes.

FORAN: You feel pretty much an intimate friend of Jerry Rubin's too?

GINSBERG: Over the years, I have learned from them both.

FORAN: Your Honor, I have to get some materials to properly carry on my cross-examination of this witness. It will take me some time to go downstairs to get them.

COURT: How long will it take?

FORAN: I think at least several minutes, Your Honor. Ten, fifteen minutes.

COURT: Are you suggesting we recess?

FORAN: I would think possibly yes, Your Honor, because I would just get back here and get started . . .

COURT: You mean recess until the afternoon?

FORAN: After lunch.

COURT: All right. We will go until two o'clock.

WEINGLASS: Your Honor . . .

KUNSTLER: Your Honor, we have witnesses leaving the country this afternoon who are presently here. One is leaving tomorrow morning and must testify now or we lose him forever, and the other has to return to the West Coast.

COURT: I have granted the request of the Prosecution.

KUNSTLER: We asked for five minutes two days ago in front of this jury and you refused to give it to us.

COURT: You will have to cease this disrespectful tone.

KUNSTLER: That is not disrespectful; that is an angry tone, Your Honor.

COURT: Yes, it is. I will grant the motion of the Government.

KUNSTLER: You refused us five minutes the other day. Why the different treatment?

COURT: I will not sit here and have you assume that disrespectful tone to the Court.

KUNSTLER: This is not disrespectful.

COURT: Yes, it is.

KUNSTLER: I am asking you to explain to the Defense which claims it is getting different treatment, why a simple request for five minutes was not granted.

COURT: I have admonished you time and again to be respectful to the Court. I have been respectful to you.

KUNSTLER: Your Honor, this is not disrespectful to anybody but . . .

COURT: You are shouting at the Court.

KUNSTLER: Oh, Your Honor.

COURT: Shouting at the Court the way you do.

KUNSTLER: Everyone has shouted from time to time, including Your Honor. This is not a situation . . .

COURT: Make a note of that. I have never . . .

KUNSTLER: Voices have been raised.

COURT: I have never shouted at you during this trial.

KUNSTLER: Your Honor, your voice has been raised.

COURT: You have been disrespectful.

KUNSTLER: It is not disrespectful, Your Honor.

COURT: And sometimes worse than that.

GINSBERG: Ommmmmmm.

KUNSTLER: He was trying to calm us down, Your Honor.

COURT: Oh no! I need no calming down.

Blackout.

SCENE FIVE

Examination of Defense Witness RICHARD DALEY,
Mayor of Chicago

KUNSTLER: Mayor Daley, in one of your answers to my previous questions you stated something about your instructions to offer hospitality to people coming to Chicago.

FORAN: I object to the form of the question, Your Honor, as leading.

KUNSTLER: It's not even a question, Your Honor. It's a statement, a predicate for . . .

COURT: Well, ask the question. Don't summarize the previous evidence. I sustain the objection.

KUNSTLER: In view of what you said, do you consider the use of night sticks on the heads of demonstrators was hospitable?

FORAN: Objection, Your Honor.

COURT: I sustain the objection.

KUNSTLER: Mayor Daley, do you believe that people have a right to demonstrate against the war in Vietnam?

FORAN: Your Honor, I object to the form of the question. It is an improper form of question.

COURT: I sustain the objection to the question.

KUNSTLER: Mayor Daley, on 28th of August 1968, did you say to Senator Ribicoff...

FORAN: Oh, Your Honor, I object.

KUNSTLER: "Fuck you, you Jew son-of-a-bitch, you lousy motherfucker, go home"?

FORAN: Of all the improper, foolish questions, typical, Your Honor, of making up questions that have nothing to do with the lawsuit.

KUNSTLER: That is not a made-up question, Your Honor. We can prove that.

FORAN: I ask that counsel be admonished, Your Honor.

KUNSTLER: I have the source, Your Honor.

COURT: May I suggest to you, sir, that this witness is your witness and you may not ask him any leading questions even of the sort that you proposed—especially rather of the sort that I heard part of a moment ago.

KUNSTLER: Your Honor, I have tried to reiterate ten times that in view of the nature of this witness, it is impossible to examine him and get the truth of the matter with these restrictions...

COURT: This witness is no different from any other witness.

KUNSTLER: But, Your Honor, that isn't so. He is different from any other witness. He is the Mayor of the city...

COURT: In this court he is just another witness.

KUNSTLER: Well, Your Honor, then I renew my motion that he be declared a hostile witness.

WEINGLASS: Your Honor, Rule 43(b), Federal Rule of Civil Procedure, states that a party may interrogate any unwilling hostile witness by leading questions as if he had been called by the adverse party.

COURT: The motion of the witness will be denied. The Court finds that there is nothing in the testimony of the witness that has indicated hostility. On the contrary, his manner has been that of a gentleman.

KUNSTLER: But, Your Honor, the defendants have publicly stated that they believe that he is the real culprit here.

COURT: You procured him to come to a court through a writ which was issued out of this Court. He is here. If you ask him the proper questions . . .

KUNSTLER: We are trying, Your Honor, to get to the truth of what happened during Convention Week.

COURT: You must get at the truth through proper questions, sir.

FORAN: Through the law of evidence, Your Honor, that it has taken five hundred years to achieve.

KUNSTLER: Mayor Daley, have you been at all familiar with the report of President Johnson's Commission to investigate the causes of violence at the Democratic National Convention?

FORAN: I object, Your Honor.

COURT: I sustain the objection.

KUNSTLER: Do you agree with the commission's finding that a police riot took place in the city of Chicago?

FORAN: Your Honor, I object to that. I ask the jury be instructed to disregard it and I ask that counsel be admonished for asking an intentionally improper question.

COURT: I sustain the objection because it is grossly improper. I direct the jury to disregard the last question put to the witness by Mr. Kunstler.

SCHULTZ: But, Your Honor, there is a problem here. Most of the questions are leading and we don't object to all of them but we keep on getting up and getting up. As I said before it becomes embarrassing. For people who don't know the legal rules it looks very bad for the Government to be constantly getting up. It makes it appear that we are trying to hide certain things and we just want him to conform to the proper line of questioning.

KUNSTLER: Your Honor, is this an objection or a speech, because we don't understand it.

SCHULTZ: I am begging defense counsel to ask questions properly.

COURT: Don't beg.

SCHULTZ: That is what it is, Your Honor.

COURT: Don't beg. You needn't beg. I will order them not to ask leading questions. I order you not to ask any leading questions.

Blackout.

SCENE SIX

Examination of Defense Witness DONALD PETERSON,
Chairman of the Wisconsin Delegation to the
1968 Democratic Convention

WEINGLASS: If the Court's ruling is that anything that occurred on the floor of the convention is irrelevant to this, I have no further questions, but if the Court does not make the ruling, I will attempt to elicit from this witness what occurred on the floor of the convention. I am just asking the Court what the basis of the ruling...

COURT: I am not obligated to answer that question.

WEINGLASS: Well then, we will have to go on. Now I don't want to waste this time.

SCHULTZ: Then let Mr. Weinglass, without asking a leading question, ask the witness what happened on the floor of the convention at about a certain time without suggesting...

WEINGLASS: I thought I did that.

SCHULTZ: No, Mr. Weinglass. If he asks that question...

WEINGLASS: Okay, I don't want to argue this.

SCHULTZ: I will object to that question. But if he asks it non-leading, then we can resolve Mr. Weinglass' dilemma.

WEINGLASS: Mr. Peterson, what happened on the floor of the convention at approximately ten o'clock?

SCHULTZ: Objection.

COURT: I sustain the objection.

WEINGLASS: That is incredible.

SCHULTZ: Now Mr. Weinglass has the ruling of the Court in this area.

WEINGLASS: Mr. Peterson, what happened on the floor of the convention at approximately ten-thirty?

SCHULTZ: Objection, Your Honor.

COURT: I sustain the objection.

WEINGLASS: What happened on the floor at any time that night after nine P.M.?

SCHULTZ: Objection.

COURT: I sustain the objection.

WEINGLASS: Mr. Peterson, what did you do on the floor of the convention?

SCHULTZ: Same objection, Your Honor, relevancy.

COURT: I sustain the objection.

SCHULTZ: Now Mr. Weinglass has the Court's ruling that what happened at the convention on Wednesday night is not material to this case.

Blackout.

SCENE SEVEN

NOTE: *When the Court was not in session the defendants were allowed to appear publicly throughout the country to raise money for their defense.*

COURT: It has been brought to my notice that there was a speech given in Milwaukee discussing this case by one of the defendants—not that this was the first time a speech was given about this case by one of the defendants in this trial. I want to say that if such a speech as was given is brought to my attention again, I will give consideration to the termination of bail of the person who makes the speech. I think he would be a bad risk to continue on bail. Mr. Marshal, bring in the next witness please.

DELLINGER: I made the speech.

COURT: What did you say?

DELLINGER: I made the speech. Was there anything in the speech that suggested I wouldn't show up for trial the next day or simply that I criticized your conduct of the trial?

COURT: I didn't ask you to rise, sir, and I am certainly not going to be interrogated.

DELLINGER: Why are you threatening me with revocation of bail for exercising my freedom of speech? What has that got to do with it? I am here, aren't I?

HOFFMAN: Right on.

COURT: I think it is wholly inappropriate for defendants in a criminal case to make the kind of speech that was made and the matter of bail goes beyond mere protection for the Government that the defendant appear.

HOFFMAN: I will be in Miami on Sunday with the same speech. (*Other* DEFENDANTS *name cities.*)

COURT: Did you hear that? I haven't heard either lawyer for the defendants try to quiet their clients during this trial when they spoke out, not once in four and a half months—not once.

WEINGLASS: This question of bail revocation. I think Your Honor should clarify . . .

COURT: I will determine what to do if and when speeches of a certain kind and character is brought to my attention. Free speech is not at issue here.

Blackout.

SCENE EIGHT

Rebuttal Case for the Government.
Testimony of Government Witness JAMES B. HATLEN,
Deputy Chief of Police, Chicago

SCHULTZ: Now, at approximately five forty-five, what if any announcements were made?

HATLEN: I heard an unidentified speaker announce over a bullhorn to the group that inasmuch as the march had been stopped, to break in small groups and go over to the Loop, and disrupt their normal activity, and, if possible, to tie up traffic in the Loop.

SCHULTZ: Did the defendant Dellinger say anything when this announcement was completed?

HATLEN: I do not recall him stating anything, but I did notice that he left with the head of the march, with the group that was carrying flags.

DELLINGER: Oh, bull-shit.

COURT: Did you get that, Miss Reporter?

DELLINGER: That is an absolute lie.

COURT: Did you get that, Miss Reporter?

DELLINGER: Let's argue about what I stand for and what you stand for, but let's not make up things like that.

COURT: I will not permit the obscenities engaged in or applied by Mr. Dellinger. I don't use that kind of language myself. And I don't even like to use it in court here to quote the defendant. I shall turn over a transcript to the United States Attorney, and I hereby terminate the bail of the defendant Dellinger and remand him to the custody of the United States Marshal for the Northern District of Illinois for the remainder of this trial.

KUNSTLER: He is my client and I think this is utterly . . .

COURT: This isn't the first word and I won't argue this.

DELLINGER: There's no pretense of fairness in this Court.

MARSHAL: Be quiet, sir.

DELLINGER: You gagged Bobby Seale because you couldn't afford to listen to the truth that he was saying to you. Now you're accusing me . . .

MARSHAL: Sit down, please and be quiet. Will you be quiet, Mr. Dellinger.

DAVIS: This Court is bull-shit.

COURT: There he is saying the same words again.

HAYDEN: You can jail the revolutionary but you can't jail the revolution. (DELLINGER *is knocked to the floor by the* MARSHALS *and a courtroom battle ensues.*)

DAVIS: No, I say it. Everything in this Court is bull-shit. I associate myself with David Dellinger completely 100%. This is the most obscene Court I have ever seen.

HOFFMAN: You know you can't win this fucking case. The only way you can is to put us away for contempt. We have contempt for this Court and for this whole rotten system. That is why they want this, because they can't prove this fucking case.

COURT: Mr. Marshal, will you ask defendant Hoffman to sit down.

HOFFMAN: Oh, tell him to stuff it up his bowling ball. How's your war stock doing, Julie?

Blackout.

S C E N E   N I N E

Closing Arguments

SCHULTZ: Ladies and gentlemen of the jury, gentlemen of the Defense. The Government rested its case over two months ago and it is hard to remember what all that evidence was, especially when the defendants never met the Government's case. So there was nothing to refresh you as to what the issues were, because in the last two months you have hardly heard a scrap of evidence that relates to the case, to the charges in the indictment.

WEINGLASS: Ladies and gentlemen of the jury: The Government has to prove its case beyond a reasonable doubt and you have to believe it beyond a reasonable doubt, and if you can believe the starting premise of the Government's case, that these men plotted to put themselves in jail, that they conspired to have this trial, then you could find them guilty. But I suggest to you that the whole foundation upon which this case is built, the whole structure of it, put in terms of common sense is just not acceptable as a rational proposition.

SCHULTZ: Now the first question you must ask yourselves is why would anybody want to incite a riot. Why would anybody want to incite a situation where people are beating each other, where demonstrators are beating policemen, policemen are beating demonstrators. Why would they want this? Well, in answering this question we can look at the defendants' own statements. Davis wanted the President to use troops to secure the nomination. He wanted to use violence to precipitate the National Liberation Front in the United States. Where people would rise up in anger against the government and that would be precipitated by a riot. Hayden wanted to create what he referred to after the convention as the first step towards the revolution. Dellinger said he wanted to bring the U.S. military machinery to a halt. Rubin . . . Rubin told Norman Mailer in December 1967 that the presence of 100,000 people at the Festival of Life would so terrify the establishment that the convention would be held under armed guard and the resulting violence by the establishment itself would be such that the establishment would smash the city. Hoffman stated right after the convention that he wanted to smash this system by any means at his disposal. He stated in an interview that was published that, "He wanted to wreck this fucking society." That's what he said. So while the defendants profess that they came here for nonviolence, their own statements contradict that.

WEINGLASS: Abbie Hoffman and Rennie Davis signed their names to applications in one case five months before the convention. Abbie flew here three times to meet with city officials. Rennie is here constantly meeting with them. And when they couldn't get what they wanted, what did they do, these men who wanted all this violence? They filed a lawsuit in this building, in the Federal Courthouse compelling the city who won't negotiate with them to come to court. And all this the Government would have you believe these men did while they intended to cause violence and a civil disturbance in this city.

SCHULTZ: They are guilty of coming here to incite a riot. They came here and they incited a riot.

WEINGLASS: I want to indicate to you in closing that this case is more than just the defense of seven men. It involves the more basic issue of whether or not those who dare to stand up can do so in this country without grave personal risk and I think it will be judged in that light. And I think while you deliberate on this case, that history will hold its breath until you determine whether or not this wrong we have been living with will be righted, by a verdict of acquittal for the seven men who are on trial here. Thank you.

COURT: Mr. Foran . . .

FORAN: Ladies and gentleman of the jury. These are highly sophisticated, highly educated men, every one of them. They are not kids. Davis, the youngest, is twenty-nine. These are highly sophisticated, educated men and they are evil men.

There are millions of kids who naturally resent authority, who are impatient for change, want to fix things up. There is another thing about a kid, if we all remember, that you have an attraction to evil. Evil is exciting and evil is interesting, and plenty of kids have a fascination for it. These men know how to draw the kids together and use them to accomplish their purposes. Kids in the 60s are disillusioned. They feel that John Kennedy went, Bobby Kennedy went, Martin Luther King went and the kids do feel that the lights have gone out in Camelot, the banners are furled, and the parade is over. These guys take advantage of them, evilly, and they use them for their purposes. They tried to give us this bunk that they wanted to talk about racism and the war and they wanted a counter-convention. They didn't do anything but look for a confrontation with the police. Of course, the imperfections of our life cry out for answers. They cry out for legal answers. Effective law is the greatest achievement of mankind yet and I believe most Americans feel it is not only necessary but is highly desirable. We must have law. The vision and ideals of our fore-fathers can not be corrupted by the haters and the violent anarchists. The lights in that Camelot kids believe in need not go out. These banners can snap in the spring breeze and the parade will never be over if people will remember what Thomas Jefferson said, "Obedience to the law is the major part of patriotism." These seven men have been proven guilty beyond any doubt. You are under oath to fulfill your obligation without fear, favor, or sympathy. Do your duty.

COURT: In reaching your verdict you must not in any way be influenced by any possible antagonisms you may have towards the defendants—their dress, hair styles, speech, reputation, court-room behavior or quality, personal philosophy or life-style.

*   *   *

The Contempt Citation. All eight defendants, as well as their lawyers, were sentenced for direct contempt of court.

COURT: From the outset of the trial the Court admonished and warned the defendants and their counsel to refrain from such conduct, particularly when committed in the presence of the jury. They chose deliberately to disregard such admonitions and have openly challenged and flaunted their contempt for both this Court and the system of law it represents. Particularly reprehensible was the conduct of counsel, who not only disregarded a duty to advise and direct their clients to observe the rules of this Court but participated with their clients in making a mockery of orderly procedure.

*　　*　　*

The defendant JOHN FROINES *is sentenced to six months and eight days for contempt.*

FROINES: No, Your Honor! There are millions of defendants throughout this country who still have to be charged. And neither you, nor anybody like you can punish and sentence all of them. When history is written, the men who are sitting at this table, and the people in the spectator section who stood all night to get into this courtroom, they are the heroes. What's going to happen in this country is something that a man like you couldn't possibly understand.

COURT: Crowd out of your minds that this Court ever set out to be a hero. Any judge who sets out to be a hero or all things to all peole, well, he'll be a mighty incompetent judge.

FROINES: I'm not suggesting that you're a hero, so you don't have to deny it.

COURT: No man in his profession may be perfect, but you and your co-defendants have availed yourselves of the benefits of the American federal judiciary system.

FROINES: Availed ourselves. You have that a little bit backwards, don't you? Because we didn't ask to come here.

COURT: What did you say?

FROINES: We didn't ask to come here. I would have preferred to stay where I was.

*　　*　　*

The defendant LEE WEINER *is sentenced to two months and seventeen days for contempt.*

WEINER: Throughout this trial I have sat in quiet rage over what I've seen go on in this courtroom. If I didn't stand four times and that constitutes contempt of court—I can only say to you that I feel that contempt of court very deeply, very strongly in my heart and yet I don't personally condemn you for being what you are, just as I don't personally condemn Tom or Dicky. They are technicians: they do their job for a fascist state.

COURT: I must admonish you, sir . . .

WEINER: Yes, you must admonish me . . .

COURT: I am supposed to be especially tolerant because years ago when I was a much younger man, I was a member of the faculty of the school that you—I don't know whether you still are—at least it has been suggested here during this trial that you are or were a teacher there.

WEINER: I even understand that there is a plaque naming an auditorium after you at the Law School. At latest report, by the way . . .

COURT: You are nice to tell the assembled spectators here . . .

WEINER: I tell them actually for an evil reason . . .

COURT: . . . that there is a Hoffman Hall on Northwestern University's campus.

WEINER: I tell them actually because I am suggesting it is evil.

COURT: Yes, well, perhaps those who think ill of me here because of some of the things that have been said might have some compassion.

WEINER: I'm pleased to inform you that the plaque has been ripped off the wall.

COURT: My plaque?

WEINER: Your plaque has been ripped off the wall in the auditorium. You see apparently while the board of trustees has this great affection for you, the student body does not.

*   *   *

The defendant DAVID DELLINGER *is sentenced to two years, five months and sixteen days for contempt.*

COURT: The Court has concluded its reading of the record in respect to the defendant Dellinger. The Court finds that defendant Dellinger guilty of direct contempt of court. Mr. Dellinger, do you care to say anything before sentence is imposed?

DELLINGER: Yes.

COURT: Not a legal argument.

DELLINGER: No. I want to make a statement on the context . . .

COURT: Only in respect to punishment, I will hear you.

DELLINGER: Yes. I think it relates—and I hope you will do me the courtesy not to interrupt me while I am talking.

COURT: I won't interrupt as long as you are respectful.

DELLINGER: Well, I will talk about the facts and the facts don't always encourage false respect. Now I want to point out first of all that the first two contempts cited against me concerned one, the moratorium action and, secondly, support of Bobby Seale. The war against Vietnam; the aggression against Vietnam, and racism in this country, are two issues that this country refuses to take seriously.

COURT: I hope you will excuse me, sir. You are not speaking strictly to what I gave you the privilege of speaking to. I asked you to say what you want in respect to punishment.

DELLINGER: I think this relates to the punishment.

COURT: Get to the subject of punishment and I will be glad to hear you. I don't want you to talk politics.

DELLINGER: You see, that's one of the reasons I have needed to stand up and speak here, because you have tried to keep what you call politics, which means the truth, out of this courtroom, just as the Prosecution has.

COURT: I will ask you to sit down.

DELLINGER: Therefore, it is necessary . . .

COURT: I won't let you go any further.

DELLINGER: You wanted us to be like the good Germans support-ing the evils of our decade and then when we refused to be good Germans and came to Chicago and demonstrated, despite the threats and intimidations of the establishment, now you want us to be like good Jews, going quietly and politely to the concentra-tion camps while you and this Court suppress freedom and truth. Well, the fact is I am not prepared to do that. You want us to stay in our place like black people are supposed to stay in their place . . .

COURT: Mr. Marshal, I will ask you to have Mr. Dellinger sit down.

DELLINGER: . . . like poor people are supposed to stay in their place, like people without formal education are supposed to stay in their place, like women are supposed to stay in their place . . .

COURT: I will ask you to sit down.

DELLINGER: . . . like children are supposed to stay in their place, like lawyers are supposed to stay in their places.

MARSHAL: Be quiet, Mr. Dellinger.

DELLINGER: You take an hour to read the contempt citation, you have the power to send me away for years, but you will not give me one-tenth the time to speak what is relevant by my deserts and by history's deserts as well. I sat here and heard that man, Mr. Foran, say evil, terrible, dishonest things that even he could not believe in—I heard him say that and you expect me to be quiet and accept that without speaking up.

People will no longer be quiet. People are going to speak up. I am an old man and I am just speaking feebly and not too well, but I reflect the spirit that will echo throughout the world.

COURT: Take him out.

DELLINGER'S DAUGHTER: Daddy, daddy!

DELLINGER: Leave my daughter alone. Leave my daughter alone.

DELLINGER'S DAUGHTER: Daddy, daddy . . . !

DEFENDANT: Leave that girl alone.

DEFENDANT: Leave her alone.

MARSHAL: Will everyone sit down?

SPECTATOR: Get your fucking storm troopers out of here.

MARSHAL: All right, sit down. Have a seat!

SPECTATORS: (*Offstage.*) The whole world is watching! The whole world is watching!

DELLINGER: Well, you preserved law and order here today, Judge. The day will come when you'll take every one of us.

*   *   *

Verdicts and Sentencing. "If we make non-violent revolution impossible, we make violent revolution inevitable." J. F. Kennedy.

COURT: Good morning, ladies and gentlemen of the jury. I am informed by the United States marshal that you have reached a verdict or some verdicts. I direct the clerk to read the verdicts.

CLERK: Defendant Abbott H. Hoffman has been found guilty as charged.

COURT: Mr. Hoffman, do you have anything to say before sentencing is imposed?

HOFFMAN: I feel like I have spent fifteen years watching "You Are There." It's sort of like taking LSD, which I recommend to you, Judge. I know a good dealer in Miami. I could fix you up.

DELLINGER: I feel more compassion for you, sir, than I do any hostility. I feel that you are a man who has had too much power over the lives of too many people for too many years. You have sentenced them to degrading conditions without being fully aware of what you are doing, and undoubtedly feeling correct and righteous, as often happens when people do the most abominable things.

RUBIN: You have done more to destroy the court system in this country than any of us could have ever done. All we did was come to Chicago and the police system exposed itself as totalitarian. All we did is walk into the courtroom and the court system exposed itself as totalitarian.

HOFFMAN: Mr. Foran says that we're unpatriotic. Unpatriotic. I don't know, that has a kind of a jingoistic ring. I suppose I am not patriotic. But he says we are un-American. I don't feel un-American. I feel very American. I said it's not that the Yippies hate America. It is that the American dream has been betrayed. That has been my attitude.

DAVIS: When I come out of prison it will be to move next door to Tom Foran. I am going to be the boy next door to Tom Foran. And the boy next door, the boy that could have been a judge, could have been a prosecutor, could have been a college professor, is going to move next door to organize his kids into the revolution!

DELLINGER: Our movement is not very strong today. It is not united, it is not well organized; it is very confused and makes a lot of mistakes. But there is the beginning of an awakening in this country that will not be denied because however falsely applied the American ideal was from the beginning, nonetheless there was a dream of justice, equality, freedom and brotherhood and I think that dream is much closer to fulfillment today than it has been at any time in the history of this country.

HOFFMAN: I know those guys on the wall. I know them better than you; I feel I know Adams, I mean, I know all the Adams. They grew up 20 miles from my home in Massachusetts. I played with Sam Adams on the Concord Bridge. I was there when Paul Revere rode right up on his motorcycle and said, "The pigs are coming, the pigs are coming!" I was there. I know the Adams. Sam Adams was an evil man.

RUBIN: I am glad we exposed the court system because in millions of courthouses across this country blacks are being shuttled from the streets to the jails and nobody knows about it. They're forgotten men. You see what we've done is, we've exposed that. Maybe now people will be interested in what happens in the courthouse down the street because of what happened here.

COURT: I sentence you to five years imprisonment, $5,000 fine, and the cost of prosecution.

HOFFMAN: Jefferson. Thomas Jefferson called for a revolution every ten years. Jefferson had an agrarian reform program that made Mao Tse Tung look like a liberal. I know Thomas Jefferson.

DAVIS: We are going to turn the sons and daughters of the ruling class of this country into Viet Cong.

COURT: I sentence you to five years imprisonment, $5,000 fine, and the cost of prosecution.

HOFFMAN: Washington. Washington grew pot. He called it hemp. It was called hemp then. He probably was a pothead.

DELLINGER: I only wish that we were all not just eloquent. I wish we were smarter, more dedicated, more united. I wish we could all work together. I wish we could reach out to the Forans and the Schultzes and the Hoffmans, and convince them of the necessity of this revolution.

COURT: I sentence you to five years imprisonment, a $5,000 fine, and the costs of prosecution.

HOFFMAN: Abraham Lincoln? There's another one. In 1861 Abraham Lincoln in his inaugural address said, and I quote, "When the people shall grow weary of their constitutional right to amend the government, they shall exert their revolutionary right to dismember and overthrow that government." Now, if Abraham Lincoln had given that speech in Lincoln Park, he would be on trial right here in this courtroom, because that is an inciteful speech. That is a speech intended to create a riot!

HAYDEN: The problem for those who seek to punish is is that the punishment doesn't have the desired effect. Even as Dellinger is taken off to jail for his justified contempt of this Court, his teenage daughter jumps up and fights back. The punishment only fuels the protest.

So, Your Honor, before your eyes you see the most vital ingredient of your system collapsing because the system does not hold together.

COURT: Oh, don't be so pessimistic. Our system isn't collapsing. And fellows as smart as you could do awfully well under this system. I am not trying to convert you, mind you.

HOFFMAN: We don't want a place in the regiment, Julie.

COURT: What did you say? Your sentencing's coming up.

HOFFMAN: I'm being patient, Julie.

COURT: Well, I don't—you see? He thinks that annoys me by addressing me by a name—he doesn't know that years ago when I was his age or younger, that's what my friends called me.

HAYDEN: The point I was trying to make is that I was trying to think about what I regretted and about punishment. I can only state one thing that affected my feelings, my own feelings, and that is that I would like to have a child.

COURT: That is where the federal system can do you no good.

HAYDEN: Because the federal system can do you no good in trying to prevent the birth of a new world!

HOFFMAN: I don't even know what a riot is, I thought a riot was fun. Riot means you laugh, ha, ha. That's a riot. They call it a riot. I didn't want to be that serious. I was supposed to be funny. Well, it wasn't funny last night sitting in my prison cell, a five by eight room, with no light in it—nothing. Bedbugs all over. They bite. I haven't eaten in six days. I'm not on a hunger strike; you can call it a hunger strike. It's just that the food stinks and I can't take it.

HAYDEN: ... We would hardly be notorious characters if they had left us alone in the streets of Chicago last year. It would have been a few thousand people. It would have been a testimony to our failure as organizers. But instead we became the architects, the masterminds and the geniuses of a conspiracy to overthrow the government. We were invented. We were chosen by the government to serve as scapegoats for all they wanted to prevent happening in the 1970s. We were chosen because we had a history in the 1960s of doing things that had to be stopped. If you didn't want to make us martyrs, why did you do it? You know if you had given us a permit, you know if you had given slightly different instructions, very little would have happened last year in Chicago.

COURT: I sentence you to five years in prison, a $5,000 fine, and costs of prosecution.

HOFFMAN: Well, we said it was like Alice in Wonderland coming in, now I feel like Alice in 1984, because I have lived through the winter of injustice in this trial.

COURT: The defendant Abbot H. Hoffman will be committed to the custody of the Attorney General for imprisonment for a term of five years. Further a fine of $5,000 and costs...

HOFFMAN: $5,000, Judge? Could you make that three-fifty?

COURT: $5,000 and...

HOFFMAN: How about three and a half?

COURT: ... and costs will be imposed, costs of prosecution will be imposed. Mr. Marshal...

HOFFMAN: Remember to water the plants.

CLERK: The defendant Lee Weiner is found not guilty as charged. The defendant John R. Froines is found not guilty as charged.

COURT: The defendants stand committed until the fine and the costs have been paid, the prison terms to run consecutively with the prison term or prison sentence previously imposed for direct contempt of court. Not only the record in this case, covering a period of four months or longer, but from the remarks made by the defendants themselves here today, the Court finds that the defendants are clearly dangerous people to be at large. Therefore the commitments here will be without bail. (KUNSTLER *rises.*) I gave you the opportunity to speak at the very beginning. You said counsel did not desire to speak.

KUNSTLER: Your Honor, couldn't I say my last words without you cutting me off?

COURT: You said you had nothing to say.

KUNSTLER: Your Honor, I said just a moment ago we had a concluding remark. Your Honor has succeeded perhaps in sullying it, and I think that maybe that is the way the case should end, as it began.

PHOTO COURTESY THE ODYSSEY THEATRE

On "The Chicago Conspiracy Trial"

Frank Condon

The creation of a documentary drama poses special problems to the adaptor and the director. To discover how some of these problems were attacked in creating The Chicago Conspiracy Trial *we posed a few questions to co-adaptor and director Frank Condon. Here are his written responses.*

WEST COAST PLAYS: I take it the historian sets out on a journey to find the meaning of an historical event. A theatre group sets out to find out the meaning of a text. But the mores of the historian's journey are usually different from the mores of a theatre group. Did you ever worry that the performance, in finding its own truth, would falsify the historical event?

CONDON: My utmost concern from the onset was to remain as true to the original event as possible. I insisted on maintaining the integrity of the transcripts and strove, during rehearsals, to recreate the atmosphere and tone of the original trial, as described by the reporters who covered it. I also took historical accuracy to require the audience to find itself inside that courtroom. I was especially convinced that nostalgia—that sentimental, uncritical yearning for things past—had to be carefully avoided. So I wanted the audience to experience the trial viscerally, and in the present.

Waiting to enter the theatre and being seated were all part of the event. The audience-spectators-jury entered the courtroom only after being confronted by Yippies demonstrating outside the theatre. Inside, federal marshals—instead of ushers—ensured that order and decorum were maintained. Nothing, I felt, would more effectively obliterate the sense of attending a "play" than to dispense with a clear-cut, discernible beginning. If the scuffles that took place at the feet of the audience every night were not convincing then the credibility of the text would have suffered considerably. When the audience came to its feet each evening on the clerk's order to rise, it had already been in the world of the event for some time.

I suppose in some ways I see myself as a historian, particularly in light of your question, since my intention was to illuminate the meaning of the original trial and, in the production, to let the audience experience that meaning first hand. For example, only those few who witnessed the original trial ever saw Bobby Seale bound and gagged in the courtroom. There were no photographers allowed. A black man bound to a chair and gagged inside a federal courtroom is a compelling image, to say the least. In our "courtroom" thousands experienced that image first hand. In his statement before sentencing, Abbie Hoffman described the trial as like watching "You Are There." Our re-creation of the trial could have been described with the title "You Are Here Now."

Tom Hayden called the trial "both a nightmare and an awakening." My intention throughout was for the audience in that space, whatever its political inclinations, to experience that nightmare and that awakening.

WEST COAST PLAYS: Which of the following do you feel your play resembles more closely: "60 Minutes," *Richard III,* "Perry Mason," Brecht's *Galileo,* PBS coverage of the 1980 conventions, or *Barefoot in the Park?*

CONDON: Let's see. It's not reportage, as is "60 Minutes." And it's not tragedy, as is *Richard III,* an interpretation of historical events without aid of transcripts. It's not melodrama, as is "Perry Mason"—with a clear-cut, clean-cut, hero good-guy. To be sure, we're dealing with a courtroom but that's about as far as similarities go.

I've never seen *Barefoot in the Park* in its entirety but I've seen performed some very funny scenes from it. There's lots of humor in *The Chicago Conspiracy Trial*—it's an essential element. Laughter is seldom more undecorous than in a courtroom. Justice is no laughing matter. Unless the sparring of Hoffman versus Hoffman, the attempted intimidation of Weinglass, as well as the Ginsberg scene and some of Kunstler's go-rounds with the court elicit laughter, the evening's in big trouble.

I didn't watch PBS coverage of the conventions last year. However, if our democratic process is to work at all, it seems to me the conventions should be highly competitive and have the same excitement as a sporting event (we're closing in on Brecht). More exciting, in fact, because the stakes are much higher.

More than any of the other choices, *The Chicago Conspiracy Trial* is close to *Galileo.* Both are episodic and encompass a wide range of material in a compressed period of time. Each scene in both furthers the story through treatment of a particular subject.

Brecht's Galileo is closer to being a profligate than a saint. Brecht doesn't glorify or condemn his Galileo, and so he doesn't deny the audience the opportunity to come to its own conclusions. Our courtroom also was filled with living, breathing human beings, not good guys or bad.

Even though it was difficult to avoid a biased response to the material, I strove heartily for full-dimensional characters, rather than saints, ogres or buffoons. I felt the audience should make its own judgment in this case.

Finally, the theme of *Galileo* is the same as that dealt with in *The Chicago Conspiracy Trial:* individual conscience versus state policy. It is a crucial issue, and not uniquely contemporary by any means. Sophocles had the same theme in mind when he wrote *Antigone* nearly 2500 years ago.

WEST COAST PLAYS: In shaping the script what liberties did you take with the material?

CONDON: Clearly there are elements in our adaptation that are different from the actual event. Len Weinglass commented upon our first run-through that it was an exciting evening throughout, whereas most of the original trial was pretty boring. Since there are about five and a half months of transcripts and the evening was to run about two and a quarter hours, we decided to leave out all the boring parts.

We also left out some exciting parts. In particular, when one of the defendants was forcibly taken into custody and Kunstler, in tears, banged his head against the bench and cried, "Take me too!" Those who were there said this was immensely affecting, but we were unable to make it convincing, so left it out of the evening. I believe no one would have bought it in the re-creation.

In putting together a workable dramatic evening, some shaping of the material was necessary. The chronology of some events was rearranged for structural reasons, and the names of some government witnesses were changed when testimony of two witnesses was combined.

Some of the major elements we stressed in editing and shaping the transcripts were the following:

—The early struggle for control of the courtroom, culminating in the running battle between Kunstler and the judge—this isn't resolved until well into the second act.

— The rise of Weinglass from a relative neophyte to a hardened veteran by the end of the evening.

— The concentration in each act on a particular defendant as
central victim.

The first act revolves around Bobby Seale, though in actuality
Seale was removed rather early in the trial. Extending Seale's
presence through the act gave it a dramatic spine as well as a
great curtain.

The second act is David Dellinger's, although Abbie and Ginsberg were brought to the forefront when needed.

The end of the original trial was filled with speeches and rather
than put the audience through fifteen successive monologues, we
decided to interweave them. We felt certain that by that time the
audience would welcome a leap out of chronological time. Abbie's statements prior to his sentencing seemed to be the perfect
catalyst for those of the other defendants, as well as a great finale.
His reference to the founding fathers was irresistible. Who could
deny the potency of those "guys on the wall," Washington, Lincoln, Adams and Jefferson, who'd been staring at us all evening
in silence? Jefferson's statement on the true spirit of patriotism
summarizes our intention with *The Chicago Conspiracy Trial,*
"The strength of a Democracy is only as great as the enlighten-
ment of the People."

Camp Shepard: Exploring the Geography of Character

Scott Christopher Wren

Sam Shepard conducted a four-week-long playwrights' workshop as part of the Bay Area Playwrights Festival III, held during the summer of 1980 in Marin County, under the artistic directorship of Robert Woodruff. The Festival received more than 800 scripts from across the nation, mounted full productions of four plays, gave eight staged readings and arranged numerous other special events.

West Coast Plays asked Scott Christopher Wren, one of the invited participants in the workshop, to record for us the progress of the event and to give a sense of the playwright as mentor. He wishes us to note his gratitude to the Festival staff and in particular to Michelle Swanson, Special Projects Director, who made the workshop go smoothly and who diligently tape recorded all the sessions.

The other invited participants were Phil Bosakowski, Dan Coffe, Bennett Cohen, Michael Corrigan, Kee Fricke, Dyke Garrison, Martine Getty, Barbara Graham, David Henry Hwang, David Kahn, Michael Lynch, Leland Meister, Kevin Ottem, Susan Rivers, Deborah Rogin, Robert Seigel, John Williams, and Elizabeth Wray.

Camp Shepard: Exploring the Geography of Character

Scott Christopher Wren

Day 1: June 30

A motley assortment of playwrights and Michelle Swanson of the festival staff in a circle on the grass. We are at the San Francisco Theological Seminary (in Marin), no theologians in sight. A few exceptional old Gothic buildings loom up on the hill. It's sunny, there are insects, a quiet which feels like a deserted campus. The belltower punctuates the hours passing. It's ten o'clock, obviously too early for many of us, considering the forty-five-minute commute from the city. No coffee, no Shepard and no idea yet what we are going to be doing.

I grew up only about a mile from here but haven't been back in years, so the trip over was eerie, filled with memories. Used to drive these streets in a beautiful '57 Chevy convertible, black with red interior, sounded like an inboard. Finally blew up on me. We don't look particularly like writers. The shapes, sizes, haircuts and clothing suggest countless sensibilities. Could be theologians for that matter. I wonder what Shepard has cooked up. Our invitations are wonderfully descriptive: "a writer's workshop." I hope it's not going to be a "what do *you* want to do?" event, for "get some coffee" is the profoundest thing I'll say today. I'm very conscious of the fact that I am supposed to write something intelligent about this workshop. I've got my pen and pad out, ready; haven't felt this expectant since my first class in college.

Shepard arrives around ten-thirty. Michelle turns on the tape recorder. Pause. "Hi," he says, squatting and lighting an Old Gold (must have to hunt to find them). I make a few notes. Cowboy boots, blue jeans, blue T-shirt, green and black checkered jacket, looks like something from the L. L. Bean catalog. Very matter-of-fact except for the reflecting sunglasses. He runs his hand through his hair, boyishly, and asks us what we want to do in the workshop.

Oh god, there's the question. My mind goes blank instantly. A long silence, a few tentative comments. Everyone's pretty nervous.

Finally Shepard says he is interested in exploring character, pursuing the mystery of character. What do you mean by mystery, mister? I feel an occult specter rising. Matter-of-factly, someone says that a character is what is in a play. Some appreciative chuckles. Shepard smiles, "Sure, but if that's the whole ballgame we can all go home today." He says that developing characters is a process of coming in touch with *voice*. "Voice is the nut of it," he explains. "Character is an expression of voice, the emotional tone underneath. If a writer is totally connected with the voice, it will be in the words." He emphasizes that the best resource playwrights have to draw upon is their own experience—not just emotions and thoughts but actual sensation. We spend a lot of time talking about what Shepard calls the language of the body. In other words, what it feels like to be "inside" a character. Thus, the concern for actual words, dialogue, etc. becomes secondary; the real struggle is to hook up with voice, to write from inside the character drawing upon our own experience. As Shepard says: "Dialogue and words don't invent characters. It's the other way around. Characters invent dialogue. The *mystery* is that you don't know what they're going to say next. It's not a formula, but a sensitivity to initiating the next lines, a process of *listening*. You've got to follow the story and not push it in some predetermined direction." By this he doesn't mean that the writing process is arbitrary. Rather, it's getting in touch with a certain movement, when you instinctively know it's going in the right direction. He believes that the role of technique comes through precision—not letting one's characters run wild, but exercising a control over the forces working in a play. However, what is important is writing from the moment happening in the play, rather than proceeding in accordance with some airtight formula.

The heat in Marin is a new experience so we move under the redwoods. "Want to do some writing?" he asks. The ayes have it. Try a monologue, no more than half a page, writing in the first person present, describing the sensation of the body. Huh? He emphasizes it shouldn't be a description of what we feel or think about it, but a coming in touch with the actual experience. There are a lot of questions, clarifications, etc. until we think we've got the idea, and then we fan out over the lawn, finding our spots, to write. It's an odd sensation, just sitting down and "writing," at first very self-conscious. Then after half an hour we regroup. Nobody wants to read first. Finally, someone takes the dive. The pieces go in all kinds of directions. Some of us have mistakenly assumed first person present meant writing about our bodies now. That didn't go too far. Most of the pieces sound too clever and witty—contrived would be a compliment—all of us hoping to look good. It's awful, but Shepard's generous, non-judgmental style takes the pressure off. "Look," he says, "you're all here because you can obviously do something right, so let's not waste time on things that you can already do well. The point is to try and explore some new territory." And now he asks the killer question for the first time: "What is the voice there?" We don't yet know how familiar this will become. In my notes I have "VOICE" in large capitals with a box drawn around it.

Day 2: July 1

We gather in the shade. As the sun climbs, our circle imperceptibly moves across the field, trying to stay under its shrinking protective cover. Nobody knows anybody else's names and Shepard never mentions it, so we pick them up as we can. He thinks the material from yesterday was too general. It wasn't specifically about a sensation. Today he suggests the same format, a short monologue—don't ramble on—in the first person present. But this time we should take one of the senses and really put ourselves inside it, so that it's very clear what sense is being expressed. Shepard emphasizes this several times. Have one specific sense come into the foreground, and let the voice be expressed through it, as opposed to the general attitude of, say, "I feel hot." As the pieces are read it's clear we are getting closer. Michael Lynch takes the experience of smell:

> I got out my old cornet the other day. Its leather case was dusty and it made me sneeze.
> I opened the case and the horn inside—the horn that I had loved so much at 13—had mildewed and it stank . . . stank like death and stagnant as a cadaver. I picked up this old, dead friend and its familiar brassy smell and valve oil reawakened a music in my nose that made my friend come alive again—the patina, the silver mouthpiece, the brass bell that never sounded like Bix Beiderbecke no matter how hard it tried.
> Any my once long-dead and decayed friend was momentarily full of life with smells of my youth.
>
> —*Michael Lynch*

Shepard comments that this piece really brings you into the moment, but urges even more simplicity. "Don't explain it, but draw us more into that sense of being there with the horn." Several other pieces are read, two about working with wood. Shepard asks how this experience would be expressed by someone who didn't know the vocabulary of carpentry. He points out that "the part of you that doesn't know all those terms is the part relating to the experience of the wood and that's the part you want to speak." The experience was captured in the pieces but the language still stands out and doesn't do the experience justice.

Then there's another piece using the sense of touch:

> He kicked off the blanket getting up.
> A draft lifted the sheet as the door closed.
> My feet poked up, marooned now. Rigid.
> There was no chance of reaching them
>   through all that ice.
>
> —*Susan Rivers*

Again, the piece puts you in the moment. Shepard says that often, if you're specific enough, in this case using the sense of touch, you'll create vivid pictures. But he goes on to say that the reference to "ice" at the end of the piece tends to lift it into metaphor, where it becomes an idea and comments on the situation. He emphasizes that we don't need to make things important. If they are specific enough, the situation is already important.

What excites Shepard about writing is when it's discovered in the moment. "An accident happens which takes you totally by surprise," he says. "It's like discovering gold. The more surprises you can welcome into your writing, the less you need to worry about technique." He eschews formulas in favor of discovering one's own rules in writing. "After all, if writing isn't an adventure, why do it?" But he cautions, "There's no reason to flog yourself at the typewriter. Writing has to be fun and exciting. And the more you go on the adventure, the more amazing it gets, the more it leads into unknown territory."

The discussion is suddenly interrupted by a few drops of rain, which in seconds develops into a torrent. We scurry, papers flying, into the theatre and take refuge upstairs, attempting to read the rest of the pieces above the howl of the bandsaw. It seems hopeless, then suddenly we decide to compete directly. The next monologue is shouted from the balcony to the crew below. The noise stops for a few seconds as they gaze up at us, but it's only a momentary victory as another piece of wood is slammed through the saw.

Phil Bosakowski and Sam Shepard.

Towards the end of the day someone comments on how difficult it is to write totally from your experience. Shepard responds that this kind of writing is tougher because you are always on the line, "You have to get in there and discover what the experience is." Working in this way opens up the possibility of finding brand new material, building on real experience rather than something outside of you, relying only upon your imagination. As he puts it, "Imagination only takes you so far, as far as your experience goes. It isn't a question of having to write about ourselves, but of contacting in ourselves the elements—forces and tendencies—that are characters. The voices of a lot of external-world characters are inside you," he explains. "For example, when you write about a nun, it's not your 'idea' of a nun, it's the nun inside of you." This is puzzling and someone asks where imagination comes in. "If you put yourself in the place of a character, that's already an imaginary act," he responds. "But once you're there you have to start dealing with the experience of the situation. For instance, if you're writing about a nun on a train, that's imaginary. Then you're got to draw upon all your train experiences—what it sounds like, how it feels and smells. But if you remain in the imaginary—'What would happen if'—you're not going to go very far with it."

The workshop never veered off this course. We approached everything from the senses, from being inside the character and listening, letting the experience itself generate the language. While none of us were particularly clear as to where this was leading we were willing to give it a try and see what happened. But not without some teeth-clenching. While most of us had been through productions of our work and hardly felt like amateurs, in this situation our production credits won't buy us a pencil. Stripped of my familiar devices and in Shepard's presence I feel incredibly self-conscious, the fledgling writer, baby playwright.

Day 3: July 2

Someone's turned the goddamn sprinklers on so we meet inside today. It's strangely claustrophobic. The openness of the field seems a lot more appropriate to what we're doing. The tension in the group is easing up. People are beginning to trust themselves more and to take some risks in the exercises. Every day a piece or two really hit. You can tell immediately when one's been written from inside the character. When it happens, it's exhilarating, if not a bit unnerving. Shepard will say something like, it's nice, it's in there, it's hot or it's beautiful. But when you miss it you get the by-now fatal line, "Where's the voice coming from?"

There is a long discussion that starts off on the topic of metaphor. Shepard has been discouraging it because he frequently finds it used as an escape or a crutch. "There is the tendency to trade in experience itself for language which never really captures it and ultimately cheats the experience." The point gets even more ominous when Shepard says he feels that this is a problem with living as well as with writing. We are always referring our experience to something else, as in "this reminds me of..." "There's a sense of hardly ever living in the present, and this kind of nostalgia comes through in the writing." Shades of "be here now," perhaps, but the theatre lives or dies on the basis of its immediacy. Someone rises to the defense of metaphor and Shepard responds by saying, "Sure, experience reverberates metaphor. But you don't search for the metaphor, but rather for the experience." "But Shakespeare's plays are full of metaphor," someone else comments. Shepard responds by saying Shakespare was a kind of saint who was able to penetrate his experience to the very core. "He traveled very far in himself to find it. The language didn't come out of thin air, it came out of a tremendous search, a religious experience. This kind of search begins from the simplest place possible and grows, gradually moving into larger territory. While a writer has to have big stakes, he can't gamble beyond his possibilities. You can't throw down three thousand dollars if you don't have it." Someone points out that this is a metaphor... laughter.

Shepard points out that language isn't a barrier or a handicap; it's a tool. But often writers don't understand true power. Rather than capturing experience, they become entangled in the literary resonances of their own rhetoric and end up intellectualizing the experience out of existence. The real challenge is to have no fat to it, he explains, to cut right to the bone. "Language has to be discovered, not structured. There are modes of expression lying dormant and every once in a while something is triggered and they become accessible to us. We need to learn how to open that channel."

The discussion winds down and we try an exercise. The familiar set-up: first person, present tense, one sense predominant. But this time another element is added: a specific place. Not an abstract place, but a real one. It could be the interior of a car, a closet, a living room, an open field, whatever; but that one predominant sense should tell us about it. Two pieces were right on target. The first by John Williams:

I don't like bright ultraviolet colors, but they're everywhere on this one section of street. What am I doing here?
It's Friday night and I know this is the way it is every week.
Christmas lights, but no Christmas presents. First Union Bap-
tist Church in yellow neon, Chinese American Café in green,
the Sportsman Inn in blue. Leonard's Barbecue Pit in smoke
gray, red amber, the meat cooking, steaming up the windows;
the smoke rising out the door and the neon cracking.

I don't like the colors but the neon keeps humming and
cracking. I keep looking up and I almost run into someone
who is upset about me stepping on his new shined shoes. But
I don't hear him, I see "Notary Public" reflecting off the
shine. I look into his face to apologize, but I see Olympia
Beer off his forehead. He walks on and I look up. I don't like
bright ultraviolet colors.

I walk along almost coming to the last group of neons. I see
a woman standing at the corner against a wall. A sign over her
head says, "Clay's Fine Meats."

—*John Williams*

Shepard notes that there's the sense of one impression leading to
the next, that they aren't just stuck on to each other. Then a second
piece by Bennett Cohen:

Salt. Moist salt. Sweat. Off my mustache. Sweat beads in fat
drops, curls over my lip and slides onto my tongue, wind-
whipped dry by air too thick to breathe. And sand. (*Spits.*)
And sand. (*Spits.*) And I spit . . . (*Spits.*) sand . . . (*Spits.*) each
time I say . . . (*Spits.*) sand . . . (*Spits.*) sand . . . (*Spits.*) whipped
up by this goddamn Santa . . . (*Spits.*) Ana.

—*Bennett Cohen*

Commenting on the rhythmic structure of the piece, Shepard
finds it very musical without being a device. A little discovery has
been made. He notes that you can feel the pieces that jump out
into the air, are alive in the air, as opposed to the ones that linger
on the page, more to be read than spoken. Quite true but it's not
very consoling to me. My piece didn't even linger. It died abruptly.
About halfway through reading it I had an awful sinking feeling.
There's a long ugly silence after I've finished. Am I missing something? I know other people have connected, but I still can't get "inside." Maybe I'm trying too hard, searching for it instead of letting
it come. Maybe. We'll see.

Day 4: July 3

A routine is developing by now. Ten o'clock doesn't seem *that* early, and we've got carpools organized. Eerie to leave the city at nine-thirty, cold and foggy, but once into Marin we hit the sun country, blue skies, Mount Tamalpais. All of us are rapidly developing suntans. It's getting difficult to figure out which locale is really the movie. If summer is happening at all it's definitely not in San Francisco. Then there's the problem of coping with things on the domestic front. The workshop is taking its toll on my general state of organization and tactical planning. I'm incapable of running errands, throw bills into an unopened pile, forget appointments and never vacuum. Although somehow I'm keeping up with the laundry. The emotional highs and lows of the workshop are felt with equal intensity. No in betweens—either wanting to celebrate or pull the sheets over my head.

Today we have very little discussion. Shepard asks us if we've been influenced by certain styles in theatre, or by any writers or particular plays. The responses run the gamut, but a lot of people start off with: "Of course, Beckett." We move on. An exercise. This time in the third person. A specific place, but still from the point of view of being inside, under the skin of a character. Using sensation, we write pieces descriptive of action. Confusion. Third person but inside? Action? How long? Still one sense? Okay. We scatter, with about 35 percent comprehension. Elizabeth Wray has an evocative piece:

46th and Broadway

She's behind the bar. It's Monday. She's pouring Chivas for Bernie, the Bond's Clothes salesman. She's safe. Out the plate glass window Seventh Avenue's gone home. Walter the Cook's downstairs sniffing coke before the movie rush. She's the boss. The wood bar holds the world in place. She's on stage and feeling right. She cut her hair last week so Charlie the Manager wouldn't say one more time: "Meet our California bargirl." She's thinking how she's got it made behind the bar. Her fear of being shot down from behind replaced by all the cool bottles pouring through her into all the various thirsty Broadway mouths. She remembers how Thursday night she read *Harmonium* on a break and watched Mick Jagger drink Bud and kiss a lady with thin lips. It broke her heart. She's pouring Chivas for Bernie. Her sleeve's more

tailored than it was last week. Bernie yells: "Hey!" Some
little kid grabs her tip glass and is out the door. She yells:
"Come back here!" and "Little punk!" Bernie says: "They're
getting younger all the time." And goes home to remind the
wife. She laughs. She puts another tip glass behind the ne-
glected California wine.

—Elizabeth Wray

But most of the rest of them are flat. Shepard talks about one of
the pieces, saying it "went up in your head," away from sensation to
commenting on it. We are slowly getting the message. Another
issue surfaces—the difficulty we have as writers reading our own
work, in that it's possible to give the piece so many different color-
ings. Shepard notes that sometimes the real voice in the writing is
covered by the attitude of the reader, but if a piece is true, an actor
should be able to get close to how it should be read. He emphasizes
that this is an active process of discovery, in which the playwright
can also learn from the actor.

A few more pieces are read. Shepard is having trouble with
them. "I think I led you down the wrong path." (Laughter.) He
proposes a more specific exercise. "Imagine one actor moving on
stage and describe his or her actions. Still in the third person, but
from inside the character, like writing stage directions. But don't
comment on it. No short stories or prose pieces. Just try to get in
touch with the sensation. If we write narrative things, we can go to
Australia, anywhere, so this time let's have everybody writing in
the same territory, on a stage." He emphasizes again not to embel-
lish with ideas, but to strip down to pure action. We get it, and
today it's my turn to make a discovery:

A door opens, upstage right. It creaks. A man is standing
there, looking straight ahead, blank expression, hands at his
sides. He runs his left hand through his hair, then scratches
the back of his head, slowly. He puts his hand down to his
side. (*Pause.*) He burps. (*Pause.*) He slowly looks down at the
tennis shoes he's wearing. (*Pause.*) He bends halfway down to
tie them, then freezes . . . then straightens back up. He's looking straight out into the room now. His right hand checks his
zipper. It takes him a while to find it. It's down. He clasps it
with his fingers, still staring straight ahead, expressionless.
(*Pause.*) He zips it up. (*Pause.*) He smiles. (*Pause.*) He closes
the door very slowly. It creaks. Blackout.

—Scott Christopher Wren

Shepard comments that there is a real sense of following the action from inside, such that the accidental gesture has purpose. It's no longer accidental because it's witnessed, followed very carefully from moment to moment. I'm elated. It's the first time all this "getting inside the character" business has really hit home. I had an incredibly vivid feeling of being *in* that character on stage, rather than outside observing and documenting the action. Thus, looking through his eyes, I wasn't thinking up what was going to happen, but was simply experiencing it as it *did* happen. Obviously that communicated itself to everyone else in the reading. Shepard observes that when one of the pieces is connected you get the feeling that the next moment will come without having to make a big deal about it, whereas other pieces seemed forced, one action on top of another, with no space in between. I begin to understand how much stronger writing can be when it's based in experience and not imagination. It's a concrete, perceptual reality—like you're *there* in it. There's nothing mystical about writing in this way.

Day 5: July 4

The workshop's been named Camp Shepard, and naturally, as with every other major and minor contemporary event, we have to have T-shirts. It isn't that we're getting sentimental, but it does feel like summer camp—fresh air, sunshine, redwoods, with Sam as camp counselor. We are also gradually associating names with faces. Instant coffee has appeared, though sugar and cream are still scarce, and we stir with any available screwdriver. All we need now are cabins and a swimming hole, a candy machine and campfires.

Today we talk about the playwright's relationship with actors and directors. Shepard thinks it's very valuable to direct your own work, even if you fail miserably. He feels that in establishing a relationship with actors, a playwright can learn a great deal from their attempts to come to terms with the material. This relationship isn't one of leadership for Shepard, but rather a reciprocal process, a dialog of trying to see and understand the material. Working as a director, Shepard says, authorship suddenly becomes secondary and he feels that anybody could have written his play. The playwright's concern with how the actors realize the material becomes the director's performance problem of how they can exercise their creativity between the material and the audience. Shepard says forcefully that playwrights have been duped by producers, agents and the press into thinking that they shouldn't direct their own

material because they're not objective. "That's bullshit," he de-
clares.

The ideal situation, in Shepard's view, is to work with a director
after having had directing experience yourself, for then you are
able to understand more clearly the director's and actors' problems.
Referring to Robert Woodruff, who has directed a number of his
plays (and is artistic director of the Bay Area Playwrights Festival),
Shepard notes that "We've found a way of working without a lot of
secretive stuff like 'Let's not let the actors hear this.' I've been
looking for seventeen years for that kind of situation." Finally he
emphasizes how important it is for a playwright to work closely on
a production, saying that "the greatest writers in the world are performed badly because they're not there."

The discussion changes course and Shepard says he thinks it's
important to read the classics, although he didn't always think so.
He confides, "I first read those Greek guys about ten years ago. I
couldn't believe it. It was incredible stuff. But there are still writers
that I just can't get into although I feel a moral obligation to read
them." "Like who?' someone asks. "Like Chekov," he says smiling.
"But that isn't saying he didn't do something," he adds over loud
laughter.

Shepard feels strongly about the importance of history, particularly American history, which can be very informative to a playwright. He mentions the Indian wars; the Louisiana Purchase. "And
the history of California," he adds with genuine fervor, "is amazing,
just amazing!" Someone asks if this is his Fourth of July pitch.
There's laughter. What time are the fireworks?

He goes on to say that he senses a change from the sixties, when
there was an embarrassment about American history, as if we could
somehow cut ourselves off from the past. "The times are now so
devastating that people are getting hungry for explanations and are
starting to question the events which have led up to the present."

But he also cautions us that the meat is in the microcosm, by now
a familiar theme to us. "The more you penetrate into the smallest
thing, the more it sends off sparks to the biggest." He feels that this
is the goal but that it's usually approached backwards—beginning
with the grand thesis. He emphasizes that writers have to begin
with what they know and one of the best places is the body, because
the body is relating to everything and it is grounded in experience
rather than ideas.

Another exercise. Find a place in the area and sit down, start to sense your body and write in detail about all the movements and sensations occurring in the moment, but write it in the third person. Why the third person? He doesn't say. The exercise is difficult because once you start to concentrate you realize how much is really going on around you all the time, how much is filtered. There's the added problem of struggling to keep opinions and evaluations out of the writing. Also, across the field a baseball game is just beginning, stealing focus. David Kahn's piece expressed this frustration:

> He doesn't like this exercise, but that's thinking, that's of the mind and he's not supposed to write of that. (These pants are hot, I have to pee, I want a coke.) He wonders what he's doing here, and yet he enjoys it, like *having* sex before you've *heard* of it, but no: it's sensation he's after. (I can't take off my pants; the sun feels terrific on the rest of me; the inside of my mouth feels like it needs mowing...) He almost says aloud, "We're all grown-ups; does this make sense?" but he has a sense of County, and of State. It must be state of mind. Don't think. He doesn't like this exercise. (The baseball bat is made of metal; I've got a headache; they'll hit me on the head.) It's the word "exercise" he doesn't like. They're going to hit me with that fucking baseball. (I'm hung over, haven't had a drink in three years. Is that sensation? If it isn't mine, does it count? A contact hangover. My arms are wet; that feels good. There's a breeze; the others will write about that. I lost my tense. I lost my sense.) Here comes the ball.
>
> —*David Kahn*

Shepard responds by saying that the point is not to avoid thought but to realize how much it dominates and covers up our experience. Susan Rivers' piece seems to come closest to what Shepard was after:

> Through the windshield the world is pitted, trees and cars covered with a fine grey fall-out. She sits in her personal shelter, protected from the elements. She fans herself with a noteook and that small movement rocks the chassis just enough to start the keys swinging from the ignition. Clack. The keys strike the chain and settle back. It is very still here—someone sitting in the passenger seat beside her may say it is completely still—but they would be wrong. Through the soles of her feet at the base of her spine, she feels the tiny

lift of the car from its axles in the breeze, a settling of the
emergency brake. She has only to reach forward and click the
key to the right, pass her foot to the clutch and shift—
smoothly, knowing just when the clutch will engage and the
car will move on to the road. The keys swing to remind her,
she can always get away.   *—Susan Rivers*

Somebody remarks that the great thing about the exercise is that
we got to choose where to sit. But someone else complains that all
the cars driving by distracted him and that it was hard to shut them
out. Shepard responds adamantly that the point is exactly that—
including the cars. They are in our world and if we exclude them (at
this point a jet plane passes overhead with deafening sound; Shepard has to stop; laughter) we start getting into preference. Someone asks, "But don't you have to be selective?" Shepard answers,
"Sure, but that's the cart before the horse. To be selective means
you already have material available to you. But what's the material?"

Week Two

Shepard is in L.A. for a week and various people come in to discuss
visual theatre, screenwriting and directing, among other topics.
Chris Hardman of Snake Theatre probably tantalizes the group the
most by his plea to throw out our typewriters and pick up paint
brushes. His manifesto is delivered from the far end of the room.
There is a long piece of butcher paper unrolled across the floor. He
starts by putting his feet on the end of the paper, then picking up
the section in front of him and reading, walking over the already-
read sections. During this time, Hardman never looks at us but
moves across the stage, speaking to a TV camera, which we see on
a monitor in front of us.

Snake Theatre is a visual theatre group, making extensive use of
masks, dance and music. Hardman sees no very compelling reason
to write naturalistic plays for the theatre, when television and film
can do so much better. Thus, he feels that theatre is suddenly
thrown back on itself because audiences are less attracted to a
theatre where characters spend most of their time talking.

People listen to his broadside attack barely taking a breath. Then
the eruption. People are upset, hell, angry . . . hostile . . . and rally
to the battle cry: "Defend language!" After a week of confirming
our mission as writers Hardman comes as a jolt to some nervous
systems. A few people storm out. The discussion rages. We write

plays because theatre's *live,* because film is a director's medium, because TV is flat, because we don't want to live in L.A.!

Still, Hardman drives a message home. It is important to remain aware of these other forms and to be able to think visually, especially to pay attention in our writing to action and movement in three-dimensional space (I'm reminded of Shepard's stage direction exercise on Day 4), and most of all to remember theatre's a live medium. It's very easy to write something into the ground, to kill it with a lack of action.

Day 11: July 14

Today, with Shepard's return, we graduate to brewed coffee and dialogue. I'm going to start bringing my own cream. They *always* run out. First, gathering on the large Playhouse porch, Michelle Swanson brings out a script box and says that if we're interested in reading each other's plays, we can check them out. Jesus, these people write actual plays? I'd almost forgotten. After selecting today's spot on the lawn, we begin to talk about attitude in characters. Shepard feels words are manifestations of shifting attitudes, and you can hear when a character is written from only the head of a playwright, as opposed to the playwright's being in touch with the pool of attitudes going on underneath that character. Attitudes as temperature, emotional tones, not the generalized attitudes or outlooks on life which, in a great deal of writing, defeat themselves, lacking specific textures, levels and intonations. "Big" emotions in particular are hard to approach directly, and can easily become false, stereotyped. Shepard views these attitudes as the notes or scales of voice. Thus, a character's voice encompasses a range of attitudes and every character has a unique range, much like different instruments, each with distinctive tonality and pitch.

The key, according to Shepard, is to listen to the attitudes closely. This is especially important in terms of dialogue, the give and take of a conversation, which he describes as "a constantly shifting, snake-like dance." He adds that, "Listening can open up the world of language, and when you're hooked up, new phrasings happen, new arrangements of lines, as opposed to when you're not listening. It's sort of like filling in the blanks." Thus the attention should be on the attitudes, not on language per se. As he explained, "What I'm interested in now is getting a little taste of a voice, in terms of attitude, and letting it start to speak. Then listening closely and trying to follow where it wants to go, as far as it wants to take you. Then giving it a rest and coming back and letting it take you further." Bouts of writing, to Shepard, have a given length of time to them, an organic phrasing, after which they become stilted. There is a certain trajectory to writing for him, and he believes it is important to stop when you're still climbing, rather than taking it too far, so that you go beyond the apex. That way, when you return to a piece of writing, it still has momentum to it. He notes he always starts out handwriting his plays, saying "the thing I like about it is that you can take it anywhere you want to go; it seems less finished, open to more possibilities."

Listening and following. But what about structure and plot? Shepard feels that if you get into the life-stream of the work, it'll tell you what its plot is. He adds, however, that he's not sure exactly what plot is anymore. There are all kinds of plots, those existing in the moment and others occurring over a long period of time, which the writer is not necessarily always conscious of. Someone interjects that he must have some idea of where a play is going. Shepard agrees that there has to be a balance, allowing a character to have a life without letting it run wild. But he notes that if a playwright is always thinking of the future, then he is shutting down the present. Working in this way takes practice, and most importantly, involves coming to a piece simply and directly, not starting out thinking it has to be a masterpiece.

Shepard explains that writers have to know the territory they want to explore, but they shouldn't perceive it in terms of "I want to write this kind of play" or "I want to make this statement." That, he believes, is self-defeating because "You can't allow something to speak if you've already decided what it's going to say." Writing a play for Shepard is like playing music. "It's exciting because you're moving into territory that is opening itself up. But it's also tough, because our language has become so corrupt, laundered, stripped of meaning. We often don't know what we mean anymore." Thus the endings of Shepard's plays are always an unknown until he gets there. He says endings are difficult for him because often the play doesn't want to end. But he feels if a play is viewed in terms of *moments,* instead of on a grand scale, ideally every breath has a beginning, middle and end to it.

What about ideas, someone asks. "The real power of ideas," he says, "is in their implications and not in their statement." He finds that ideas which evoke something are discovered in the act of writing. Although they may not ever be spoken or stated in the language, they're there in the relationships, in the context of the material. The realm of ideas too often has to do with answers, a false finality. In a play there is a continuous movement which must be allowed to live.

Shepard thinks writers are duped into believing they have to come up with answers by the intellectual community and the press. "But," he says, "it's a great mistake to assume that just because writers are involved in making pieces of work, they know what they're doing. They know to a certain extent, but to a large extent, they don't, and that's the reason they are doing it—to find out. We're always working out in the dark with a little lantern." Shepard believes that "If you are interested in writing plays, then you are interested in speaking to people. This is where ideas come in, as playwriting isn't a closet act. It's ultimately a relationship with an audience." He feels strongly that the responsibility of the playwright is to discover the life he or she is living and how that life relates to other people. But it is a relationship of being equal, not in the political sense of equality, but of being in this time together. Thus, writing is a continuous probing, and he believes that a stance of questioning can provoke much more than one of answering. In the final analysis, if playwriting isn't an act of discovery for the writer, the play won't be one for the audience.

Shepard also feels a continuing restlessness to move on, explaining that "There is a taste of satisfaction in a piece of work but it's easily swallowed. And then comes the question: okay, but what now?" He finds that each play leaves him off somewhere, with certain new questions, and this eventually feeds into his subsequent work. "This has to come with practice, with working constantly. Otherwise it sounds abstract and impractical, like I'm wandering around with some kind of philosophy." Ultimately he views writing as a journey of self-discovery, and mentioning Shakespeare and Picasso as examples, says that in this process, they were "throwing off pieces of work."

Enough. There's a pause. It's been the best discussion yet. Shepard suggests an exercise: "I thought we'd try some dialogue today." I can sense people's engines start to turn over. We're not totally sure of this "in the body" stuff, but boy can we "throw off" dialogue. Until he drops the meat axe. Four lines. Four lines? Yep, "da-dat, da-dat, da-dat, da-dat," he says, "so that it just starts to imply something, otherwise we're going to go spinning off into an epic." He's definitely onto our number.

The exercise relates back to were we began today—the question
of attitude. He asks us to spend some time preparing. Just find an
attitude that's in you already and hold it, feed it. Then once you've
got that, find its opposing factor, not necessarily a conflict, but its
counterpoint, and have the dialogue come from that tension. It's
tough, just four lines. Koans? Haiku anyone? Dyke Garrison's
piece expresses the counterpoint nicely:

> VOICE 1: God, that is really beautiful, isn't it? Gold sky
>   behind the mountains. That soft blue up there
>   with that scratch of cloud. And that—Jesus, that
>   really is the moon, isn't it? I've never seen it so
>   thin.
>
> VOICE 2: It's something to look at while you're driving.
>   Passes the time. The road between the valley and
>   the city.
>
> VOICE 1: That's just—this is right here; it takes me up in it;
>   pulls me out of the road; lets me hover.
>
> VOICE 2: Yeh, until you start to think about it. Then you're
>   right back on the road.
>
> —*Dyke Garrison*

Shepard comments that the piece seems to set up a movement to
the next moment. While there is the clear situation of driving, it's
open and the lines sort of nudge it along. Most important, the piece
invites listening as opposed to pushing it away.

   Lunch forays into San Anselmo are beginning to take place
regularly after the workshop. We debrief. Everyone has their share
of frustrations and anxieties. I drink beer, everyone else coffee. I
don't care. My day is over anyway. We only rarely discuss what
we've written. As exploratory pieces and not finished work, it
seems out of place to commend or criticize them except in the
context of exercises.

Day 12: July 15

We have a long, rambling and extremely frustrating discussion
about theatricality. We struggle to define it, but it gets nowhere. I
am silently screaming: Let's stop talking and do some writing!
Finally, Shepard takes a stab at it, saying that theatrical style obviously changes with the times, but beyond that, what is it? He refers
to sensation, saying there is the language of the body, intellect and
emotions. It is this "body language" of actual experience which is
theatrical. He adds that this perspective is not anti-intellectual, but

the problem is how to express ideas and emotions through "direct contact." Also, he adds that in the theatre, language is in the air, not on the page, and that makes it physical.

Another point comes up. That it's necessary to draw upon memory to get at sensation. That as opposed to simple recollection, it is possible to re-live the experience, so that writing opens to the senses.

At last, we do an exercise. Take a dream that's still fresh, put ourselves in the first person, and write a monologue. Shepard asks us to write only about what we actually remember, and not worry about its making sense. We should try to come into the present with it, making it as detailed as possible in terms of color, emotional tone, texture, etc., without embellishing it. Zing! Something happens, unlike a lot of the material before today, these are direct. They all give off energy. Two examples, the first by Kee Fricke, the second by myself:

On this stagnant afternoon I have my underwear dangling from a stick. I would like to sell them. This one woman with long black hair, dressed in blue jeans, selling empty wine bottles and belt buckles, says that she would like to buy them, but they are dirty. They're not really that dirty. They were just worn once and I haven't washed them since. Besides, everyone sells dirty and worn things at the flea market. She still insists that they be absolutely clean.

I move on. From behind a '65 blue Ford station wagon comes a man called The Grease Man by the flea market regulars. He tells me that he wants to buy my underwear. I tell him that I don't want him to. I am getting mad that he is so persistent. As I start to walk away, he mounts a black, 3-speed Raleigh bike and chases after me.

I'm not worried because I know that he'll never catch up to me.

—*Kee Fricke*

*　　*　　*

I've pulled into this parking lot. There are only a few cars. It's morning. At the end of the parking lot is this hill. And on this hill are all the streets I grew up on. I walk up and see all my old friends out playing. There's Leonard Greer, Ricky Sorenson, Greg Ball and even Billy Force. I'm asking them if they've seen someone, but nobody has ever heard of him, and

then I realize I'm asking them about myself. . . . Something
scares me, something so familiar I don't want to find it, and I
run back down to my car. But as I open the door I see a scarf
draped over the steering wheel. The one I gave you. And
then I notice that the bus is full of all the things I ever gave
you. I hear someone walking up behind me. I turn, it's you,
you're smiling and you tell me that you're returning all my
presents so you won't forget what I looked like.

—*Scott Christopher Wren*

Shepard is absolutely amazed. We are all amazed. But I'm more
shocked than anything. My piece just seemed to write itself. The
material just appeared, much like the sun suddenly coming out
from behind a cloud. The sense of the unknown Shepard has been
speaking of, hit me right between the eyes. But I got more than I
bargained for, as the dream really spooked me. I was shaking as I
wrote it down, having for a few minutes actually re-entered the
experience. Shepard comments that the pieces are so strong because we were drawing on such personal experience. Their impact—the way they reverberate on so many levels—seems to have
less to do with their content, as with how they were recorded, the
clarity and immediacy of the images. Someone asks whether Shepard gets a lot of his own material by deliberately delving into the
unconscious. "I don't believe in the 'unconscious.' It's all unconscious."

Day 13: July 16

I've been making a valiant attempt to keep up with the documenta-
tion of the workshop, but this "journey" has swept me up to such
an extent that my objectivity is fading. I stopped trying to take
detailed notes a few days ago. If the tape recorder fails me, I'm in
deep trouble.

Shepard shows up today on a ten-speed. A forty-five-minute ride
from his house in Mill Valley. I also notice he's not wearing his
boots, in favor of Mexican huaraches. On the porch, before we
begin, he tells a story about filming "Days of Heaven." In the night
scenes, when the fields are burned to kill the locusts, they dropped
the locusts from helicopters, then later reversed the film to give the
impression the locusts were flying out of the burning wheat. So for
several nights the actors, as well as the trucks, harvesters, etc., also
had to do everything in reverse. An eerie sight, he said, at night,
the flames and watching everyone move around backwards. It hits

me that there's a parallel with the workshop, a sense of falling backwards, into the fire.

Shepard starts the discussion by commenting on the tradition in American theatre of psychological drama—characters in crisis. He says dramatic situations don't always have to be looked at as external predicaments between characters. This approach limits the frame, as the "who" of a character does not always have to be revealed by circumstances, but can refer to an internal state. He suggests that perhaps new voices are needed in theatre, urging us to explore the huge territories not even touched upon yet. Someone asks him specifically what he means by new territory. Shepard thinks the issue is how to make characters become more than just the sum of their problems. He elaborates, saying issues raised in a play have to be more than just personal problems but everybody's problem. "Take the problem of waking up in the morning. It could be much bigger than the problem of waking up in the morning. It could be the problem of waking up in general." (Laugher.) But he cautions that this can't be imposed on a play: "It's something that happens in the course of writing. There's no formula. You have to struggle with it. But you never know. The little idea may be the big idea."

Theatre, for Shepard, is the one form open to real adventure. Emphasizing character again, he says this is the element that creates the possibility for a play to open, to move into the world of the mysterious, the unknown. He's done a " 180" in his own work. Previously he was much more interested in situation and language, but he's found everything emanating more and more from character. "If you can connect with character, you don't have to worry about the rest."

Elizabeth Wray suggests a way she sometimes works to locate or call up characters. First locate a place and describe it minutely without any characters. Think of it as a set in a theatre and make it so concrete that it will invite some of the characters who are always walking around inside all of us. We try it. Martine Getty's description is very strong, strangely haunting:

> A mattress on the floor. The bed is unmade, a wool blanket is lying half on the floor. Next to the bed is a glass, half-filled with water. A candle half-way burnt down. One book with the title *The Holy Grail*. A record player. On the chair is a birdcage with a yellow bird in it that doesn't move. In one corner is an old TV set; the image flickers black and white. A win-

dow; it is open wide. Sometimes the curtains blow up when
the wind gets caught in them. It is night. Outside the window,
mute darkness and a concrete construction. A beginning of a
bridge. Anonymous streaks of light slide over the walls when
a car passes by. The noise from tires wet on asphalt. A shred
of music far away. Somebody playing a flute. The sound of a
door being closed. Some shreds of voices, disappearing, silence. Sounds from a radio; the stations are being changed
fast.

—Martine Getty

Day 14: July 17

The workshop is rapidly becoming an institution; we've been out
on the lawn so regularly that the neighborhood dogs are now
attending. It feels like we should have homework assignments or
something. Everyone is calling Shepard "Sam" by now, and he's
miraculously getting most of our names. But we know each other
best by the work we're doing. We have the routine well developed
now. We sit, discuss, write, read and pass the tape recorder. I get
nervous when it dawns on me how many hours of tapes I'm going
to have to listen to. And today's session had the added inspiration
of being conducted over the buzz of a nearby chainsaw.

Somehow we end up talking about rewrites. Sam says he used to
believe in a "holy-art" approach of trusting what comes first as the
truest expression. But that's way behind him. He confides that he
first wrote *True West* (then having its premiere at the Magic Theatre
in San Francisco) almost a year ago and has since rewritten it twelve
times. He talks about working on something, leaving it and then
coming back to it, often with one's mood totally changed. You can
look at it once harshly, but then come back again in another mood
and like it. He advised not judging our work too quickly, but rather
giving it time to feed other connections. However, if it's not giving
you something after a while, rather than push it, it's better to start
something new.

Today's exercise is a take-off on yesterday's. We let characters be
drawn into the environments we described, and try to let the
dialogue be evoked from the place. Martine Getty's is again powerful, given the strong mood established yesterday in her description:

> *On the mattress, lying on her stomach, is a girl, about 28 years
> old. She is dressed in a large wool sweater, pants; she is barefoot
> and her hair is disheveled. She moves one arm to put the needle*

from the record player on a record.... A song starts.... After a
while she gives the needle a push. A scratching noise ends the
song.... A knock at the door.... She doesn't move.... Another
knock, more demanding this time. She gets up ... with a confused
movement she composes her hair a little bit.... She opens the
door.... There is an old Chinese man standing, the owner of this
hotel. His face must usually be hard, but now it is somehow
softened, concerned.

GIRL: What is it?... What do you want...?

MAN: I ... I just wanted to see if you're all right....

GIRL: Yes... yes... I'm all right.... Why?... Why do you
ask...? Yeah... I'm all right.... (*She wants to close the
door, but he steps into the room.*) What do you want?

MAN: I wondered... I saw you the last time three days
ago... I thought maybe...

GIRL: (*Interrupts.*) What's the day today?

MAN: Friday.

GIRL: Friday.... Friday...?

MAN: Yes, Friday... the third of April.

GIRL: That's my birthday...

MAN: Well,... I...

GIRL: (*Interrupts.*) That's okay...

MAN: You know, I don't have women living here very
often...

GIRL: I will be out... soon... I need a few more days...
then I move....

MAN: You can stay.... It's not that....

GIRL: It's cold here. You know that this room is always
cold.... I'm freezing to death....

MAN: (*Goes to the window.*) The window is open, that's why.
I'll close it...

GIRL: *No*... No.... Leave it open.... I need fresh air....
Leave it open... don't close it... don't...

MAN: Calm down. I'll leave it open, but that's why it's cold.

—*Martine Getty*

Day 15: July 18

The workshop seems to be taking on some "public interest," as
reporters from the papers have started observing sessions. Today
there's a video unit and someone taking a lot of still shots. This

Playwrights and percussion and friends.

attention strikes me as extremely strange, for the whole process has been so private and removed. I've lost track of how many times I've been asked, "What's the Shepard workshop like?" Ah ... it's nice, yeah, amazing... my voice trails off, unable to put my volatile reactions into a litle package. It feels similar to that awful question "What's your play about?"

As we arrive Dino (D. A. Deane)—who worked with Sam as a percussionist in *Inacoma*—has spread out a blanket on the lawn. Arranged all around him are chimes, bells, rattles, sticks, as well as a tape recorder with tapes of all kinds of sounds, as well as a flute, trombone, and who knows what else, any one of which he's able to locate in an instant. Dino takes a while to set everything up, and in the meantime some tomato "pudding" is passed around. It's so incredibly hot today, the stuff tastes like warm catsup.

Sam calls us to order. Dino works with a couple of people's pieces. First he listens to them, a pause, he readies a few instruments and tapes, and then plays as they are read again, creating a sound environment around them. This is moderately successful. Some more, some less. Dino talks about working in this way and explains that when he hears the words the first time he gets an image which is translated into sound. There's no conscious thinking involved. The sound suggests itself and an instrument says, "Me. I'm the one." In the middle of one of the pieces, the bell tower chimes twelve o'clock. Somehow it fits perfectly.

Shepard then asks Dino to improvise a piece for the writers to work from. He does a piece with four specific movements to it, about five minutes long. We just listen the first time, as it's being recorded. Then while it's being played back words and images and rhythms are called up, which we scribble down. We take twenty minutes to work these up. We return and while the tape plays we read the pieces simultaneously. I go first. Snatches of lines; moods, environments, repeated in various phrasings and intonations:

> Come here, baby. Come on.
> Come here. Close the circle. Close to me.
> I'm trying to tell you something.
> To talk to you,
> To take you to the center.
>
> Quiet. Calm down. Quiet. Calm down. Quiet.
> Calm down. Quiet. Calm down/quiet. Calm down/quiet.
> Quiet. Calm down ...

Suck your toes? Sorry!
Suck your toes! Sorry?
Sucksucksucksuck, sorry!
Suck, sorry. Suck, sorry. Suck, sorry . . .

Chop suey? Hungry? Let's eat and go. I'm a millionaire.
Hungry? Chop suey? I'm a millionaire! Let's eat and go.
I'm a millionaire . . . hungry! Chop suey? Let's eat and go!

                                          —*Scott Christopher Wren*

I finish and look up, feeling like I'm coming out of a trance, not
sure what's really happened. A pause, some smiles, something's
been triggered. Sam's emphasis on the possibilities of music finally
comes home to me in the "first person present."

Admittedly, it was a small beginning. We just touched the surface of possibilities. But it seemed as if a whole area of listening
opened up. The music created a stronger emotional environment
than when the pieces were read sotto voce, but there wasn't the
sense of anybody accompanying anybody else. Rather, the words
and music seemed to merge into one movement.

Week Four

The week is a jumble in my memory. We worked with actors from
the Festival on the pieces we'd written. They are some of the best
actors in the Bay Area, about fifteen of them, which swells our
group to over thirty. Little clusters of actors with a playwright all
over the field, going over the pieces, then coming back and having
the actors read them. The actors bring out all kinds of new associations and resonances in the work. This hits home, especially with a
few of the pieces which had never struck us as funny before. But
when read by the actors they are suddenly hysterical. The pieces
are done so many times, in so many ways and by so many people,
that by the end of the week I've practically memorized all of them.
It's a rich opportunity just to explore work, without the onus of a
production hanging over us. But it's frustrating to try to communicate what we envision without dampening the actors' own creativity.

On Tuesday Sam invited John Handy, the well-known jazz saxo-
phone player. Unlike Dino, John had never improvised with actors,
but had done a lot of work with dancers. The actors quickly moved
into a dialogue with Handy. He has such control over the alto sax
and such a lyrical sense that it seemed as if he were an actor, using

music instead of words. We tried a lot of different things: doing the monologues with the sax; having the actors do them without the words, using just *sounds* with the sax. We also worked with a couple of the pieces describing environments. Handy would get a sense of the mood suggested by our descriptions, and would play that, much like we felt characters were drawn textually into these environments. Some of the pieces really worked well. Others were more difficult. The sax was harder to work with than Dino's percussion, because the jazz associations of the instrument seemed to limit the context of the "voice." But what was strong came from the distinct voicing of the alto. It's up in a range that's almost human and is able to bring very strong emotional textures to the pieces. We didn't have enough time to explore very deeply the many possibilities suggested by the music, but at least we got an indication of some other ways of working. As Shepard put it, "to point out that we're not just stuck with pens and typewriters and talking to ourselves all the time." He compared the voicing of different instruments to character. Each instrument is so distinct that it's next to impossible to play an alto sax solo on a clarinet. So too, every character has a distinct voicing. In a way, our monologues are like little character songs.

All week Sam emphasized the importance of developing a collaborative relationship with actors, keying off of each other instead of our viewing them only as line-sayers, and their viewing us as only text-technicians. Shepard writes primarily *for* the actor, but in an active sense. He isn't interested in the actor as a marionette, for he views plays as much more than a blueprint from a writer. The actors' responsibility is to fulfill the material, but bringing to bear their own initiative, rather than being manipulated by some set vision. "There's nothing creative about that," Shepard states. "It's like playing basketball." He sees the actor's process as very similar to the playwright's—starting with almost nothing and going on a journey. But this doesn't imply a final destination either. "The idea of finality in theatre is bizarre. It's constantly changing, moving, in every performance, and if it gets fixed, it's dead."

As an active force, the actor can take a play in many different directions and Shepard believes there's a lot to be learned there. "But, too often," he says, "the approach is to fit them into a size 44 suit, even though they're a size 49."

So who has the ultimate interpretation? someone asks. Shepard responds immediately, "The audience!"

Shepard on the Workshop

I wanted to get Shepard's reaction to the workshop, so we arrange to meet on the last day in a little bookshop/café. Shepard pulls up outside in his new four-wheel-drive Scout and ambles in. He orders toast and coffee. Expresso? the waitress asks. Coffee, he replies.

I begin by asking him why he decided to lead the workshop. "To pay some dues," he explains. "If there was one thing I wanted to accomplish it was to try to inspire the writers to trust their own material, to feed the connection between their experience and their writing. And I got the sense that people in the workshop came around to the idea that their experience was valuable, not something to throw out the window or to avoid in preference to literature. As individuals we are a lot more interesting than a lot of literature. The fact is, writers' own experience is the best thing they've got going and too often they betray that for something else."

Shepard compares the workshop process to tilling the ground, noting that "if you don't do that you're not going to have much of a garden. But it's tough because, unlike actors and musicians, writers are always dealing with the awkwardness and pain of getting words down." He felt that this was successfully overcome, however, given the way the workshop was set up—its informality, out on the field, the lack of pressure, abundance of sun, etc.

I mention that initially I was very leery of the exercises, unsure whether good material could come from such a forced writing situation. But in the end I found them extremely useful, as they served to ground what might otherwise have been tortured literary discussions. The exercises also demonstrated to me that waiting for the big burst of inspiration is unnecessary. Shepard replies that his objective was "to turn people on to a way of writing that isn't so awesome, out there in the stars and theoretical. Playwriting is just as practical as making a chair. But people get hung up on the far-flung ideas and forget about getting down and writing. The biggest problem with a lot of writers is getting started, getting off the mound."

The workshop, at the very least, got that point across. Start. Begin. "The material is always in you. I think we are inhabited by charcters," he explains. "It's not necessary to have a library of notes. The material is always moving in a certain way and if you can just hook into a character it starts to feed out." He believes that it's much more practical, instead of trying to conceptualize an entire play, to bring attention to a single character who can gradually take on more and more life. "You sort of move into these beings and let the thing grow from that impulse."

Shepard gets up for a minute to go to the bathroom. I mull over the last four weeks, trying to distill its essence for one final question. None comes. Perhaps I've been too involved as a participant to be very objective. But I've gained a lot, insights into my own writing process as well as a healthy dose of self-confidence. The workshop also generated a real feeling of community among the playwrights, a sense of shared purpose as well as common problems. For me this has been a personal inspiration which has lasted well beyond the four weeks of the workshop. I was astonished that there was never even the slightest hint of competition between the writers. The fact that twenty playwrights could meet daily and keep self-aggrandizement to a minimum was itself a miraculous accomplishment.

Shepard returns to the table. "You know, the point I really wanted to get across in this workshop was that since theatre can encompass so much, you can't afford to cut yourself off from any possibilities. Gregory Corso told me something a long time ago. Someone was asking him about poetry, dividing it into little categories. And he said, 'You've got to take the whole thing on, take everything on.' "

As we are leaving I remember Shepard's description of the language of the theatre, "writing that leaps off the page and is alive *in the air.*" That phrase, I think, sums up his message.

David Kahn:

There are and were times when I am and was too shy and awkward
to have done and said the things I wanted to, but maybe there's a
good side to that: it leaves more time for what this workshop was
doing to me—the inside fight. Not a fight between Sam Shepard
and me, or the other writers and me. Just me. I'm having enormous
difficulties in *focusing* on what to write and how to write it.

Mr. Shepard (Do you realize no one has *ever* called him that?)
talked about a voice, or voices—and was pushing for us to find
our own. Out of which comes character, out of which comes
situation. And not the other way around.

Well, my goodness, my gracious: I *knew* all that stuff. It's just
that I'd never been forced into it, thinking hard about it, practicing
my preaching. It was a wonderfully useful month.

And it's not always easy to remember that you're not in a workshop to impress anybody else, or to gain approval. (Isn't that right,
Sam? Sam? Sir?) I think it's sad so many writers fizzled out when
they knew Sam wasn't coming, or their play or piece wasn't being
read or done. There was certainly more to the workshop than Sam.

But that's not to belittle what he's done for me. It's just hard to
talk about, because at this time in my writer's life, I'm in a sort of
agony. Due in large part to Sam, and the workshop. —But I recognize the value of growing pains. (Either that or I'm car sick.)

So what the seminar comes down to, for me, is a focus. It's as
though I'm a camera (Now there's a good idea for a title), and Sam
and the workshop provided a new lens, a new kind of lens. Now my
only problem is I got myself a busted camera.

—*David Kahn*

Elizabeth Wray:

Circles & Brown Grass. I show up. There's a whole lot of writers
sitting in a big circle outdoors on a huge California lawn sur-
rounded by trees. Maybe they call it a glen out here. It's more like a
field because the grass is burned brown on account of there's too
much sun. So here we are sitting in a circle—and me hating circles
and missing all the angles of conversation around a square table:
old seminar style, old East Coast, lit crit dissection, old job interview tension like I was doing just last week in New York— So here
we sit, a huge group of play-writers and Sam Shepard, looking on
this burnt-out grass just like he looked in the wheat fields in "Days
of Heaven." Already there's too much mystery.

I miss a lot the first few days because I'm trying to figure out where all these writers are from—a lot have weird accents and they're not all blond—and what kind of jobs they have that let them off from 9 to 1, Mondays through Fridays. Maybe they all change jobs and move around the country a lot like me. I find that possibility disturbing. Sam Shepard has a ranch in Mill Valley and hasn't been to New York since '74. Who says a playwright can't find happiness in the West. I miss a lot of what's being said but notice we're developing a routine.

The Routine. We spend the first hour asking each other embarrassing questions like: How many hours do you write a day? Or popular questions like: How do you incorporate musical phrasing into your work? Sam is embarrassed by questions about the *business* of play-writing. Others argue convincingly on the rabid popularity of a question such as: How do I get Joe Papp interested so's I can make a few bucks?

The last three hours we write and then discuss what we've written. I like this part because I get to go sit in the shade, finish waking up to myself scratching myself across a yellow tablet and then listen to the stories of the other writers.

The Writing. We write in small ways. Short monologs. Place and stage descriptions. Dream dialogs. Songs. We construct and inhabit the moments of our pieces of writing.

What I learn most from my summer vacation: EACH MOMENT IN A PLAY HAS A BEGINNING, MIDDLE AND END.

I also learn something about the astonishing. The astonishing in the object. The astonishing in the ordinary. Defining and re-defining the ordinary until it becomes the astonishing.

The Ballpark. By the second week I'm getting used to it. I still don't know anyone's name but our T-shirts are beginning to give us away. Every once in a while it feels downright natural to be spending five mornings a week with a bunch of playwrights. Especially when the local softball team plays on another part of the lawn. Those times it feels good, all American, really OK to be there—all of us, on the burning field, practicing our aim.

—*Elizabeth Wray*

Susan Rivers:

First week. I'm sitting in my car trying to write the exercise.
Through the glass I can see the others, dispersed under the trees
with problems of their own. I'm thinking of a day in kindergarten
when it appeared I was destined for illiteracy. We were each given a
placecard with our name printed on it and told to recopy it on a
sheet of newsprint. Long after every other five-year-old had finished and moved on to tying shoelaces I was struggling and failing.
I copied it in huge letters going diagonally, frontwards, backwards,
upside down, black and brutish like a ransom note. But each time I
took my attempts to the teacher her response was a troubled sigh
and the single instruction:

> "Between the *lines,* Susan. Why can't you see? It's got to fit
> between the lines."

Now here I sit with the blank paper having mastered penmanship
and passed into first grade but still itching to write in huge rowdy
discursive statements and similes and ironies that run right off the
page and go on marching marching marching when it's clearly so
much simpler to stick to the lines, the thought, to stay with the
task.

So I concentrate on the key swaying in the ignition, the lift of the
chassis in the breeze, trying to keep all my parts together where
they really ARE and not follow the right side of my brain as it goes
skipping off into Anywhere-But-Down-Here-On-The-Ground-
Land. Is it wrong to have been so strongly influenced by the Pirates
of the Caribbean ride at Disneyland? It probably is.

And I begin to write, watching the pen move and the key swing
but never straying very far from the paper and I complete something. Ordinary—maybe even crude. But . . . true? Yes. Coherent.
Fitting between the lines.   *—Susan Rivers*

From
The Coyote Cycle
Murray Mednick

The plays from *The Coyote Cycle* were all premiered at the Padua Hills Writers Conference and Festival of Plays, *Pointing* in 1978, *The Shadow Ripens* in 1979, and *Planet of the Spider People* in 1980. The three plays were performed together for the first time on October 10, 1980, at the Intersection Theatre, San Francisco. All productions were with the following cast:

COYOTE	Darrell Larson
TRICKSTER	Norbert Weisser
OLD SPIDER WOMAN	Ellen Blake

With props by Kim Simons

The Intersection production—the first done indoors and with artificial light—was designed by the following artists:

Set design by John Wilson
Soundtrack by Don Preston
Lighting design by Karen Musser

From The Coyote Cycle
Murray Mednick

Coyote I: Pointing

On Coyote I: Pointing

The idea for this play (and also its method) was derived from an exercise which we called "finding the spot." The actor enters a defined space, and through an effort of sensing, concentration, and alert observation, finds a "spot." It is the right spot, the only spot, and has "meaning." Once he has contacted it, he tries to express this through a process of sound and movement.

This exercise was elaborated in several ways, but most importantly: the actor's path to, and communication of, the "spot," is stalked, traced, "eaten," by his partner (TRICKSTER); having done so ("inside" and out) he takes the position of hunter, watchful for a break in the other's attention, or for any false move, and when this occurs, he "points."

The pointing was a key to the whole development of the play—it is its most pungent grammatical sign. The image for it comes from a Coyote story, wherein Coyote is mesmerized by what he thinks is a man pointing at him on the other side of the lake. He stands there for days. Finally someone comes along and tells him that the so-called man pointing is nothing but a stick in a bush.

A chief concern of ours was to find a way to achieve strong theatricality in outdoor conditions, and this led us to the physical movement and grammar of the piece and to the Coyote/Trickster myth. Obviously there were also other reasons—a sense of place, continuity; the tricky, almost ironical tone; the sometimes outrageous content. But these old Indian stories come down through us, are sifted through us, in our own particular way—we're not illustrating anything, but trying for a true, if fragmentary, mythical format in our own language—a kind of mirage which ends only because the sun goes down.

THE SCENE: *A clearing in the woods bounded by four olive trees. A rope net is spread in the tree cover above. Dusk.* OLD SPIDER WOMAN *sits against one of the trees quietly crocheting a "spider web." When the audience is seated, she blows a shrill whistle;* COYOTE *falls from above.*

COYOTE: Coyote was sent by Earthmaker on a mission, which is to destroy the evil spirits afflicting mankind. (*Pause.*) To make the waterfall come to earth. (*Makes a spiraling gesture. Pause*) He bounced around, doing the best he could. Most of the time he forgot. He made a lot of dumb mistakes. He's not good and he's not bad, but he's tricky. (*Listens.*) You've got to climb high into the mountains, way above the snow line. (*Hears something. Freezes. Listens hard. Points.*) There! (*He drops the point, but remains extremely alert.*) Coyote is a wanted man.... (*Suddenly he points in the other three directions.*) There! There! There!

A beat. TRICKSTER *comes up out of the ground.*

COYOTE: Are you a human being?
TRICKSTER: Is my body attached? Is my body attached? Is my body...? Can you see it?
COYOTE: A muddy man. A mental man.
TRICKSTER: (*Opening his eyes, feeling his body.*) I was in a place where the beings had only heads. I had to go deep into the earth to get my body back. Deep down into the ground. And keep my eyes closed and not look around.... I had to get my body back.
COYOTE: What did you see down there?
TRICKSTER: I kept my eyes closed.
COYOTE: Right. Did you feel anything?
TRICKSTER: Going down, I didn't have no body. Coming back I grew bones and meat stuck to them. My skin tightened on the heart. I could sense the pulse.... (*Stops.*) I have my body!
COYOTE: Don't scratch it. (*Referring to the ground.*)
TRICKSTER: I...
COYOTE: Don't scratch it. Leave it alone.
TRICKSTER: My bones rattle when I dance! My bones rattle when I dance! My heart has a skin! I...
COYOTE: (*Points.*) There! (TRICKSTER *assumes protective posture.*)
TRICKSTER: Did you break any bones?
COYOTE: No.
TRICKSTER: Good. That was quite an interesting fall.
COYOTE: You could see that?

TRICKSTER: I could hear it. It was like the thunder.

COYOTE: It was from another world. Way above the snow line. Coyote returns from the upper world by sliding down the spider web.

TRICKSTER: (*Looking up at the net in the trees.*) Is that what that is, a spider web?

COYOTE: No. It's twine netting.

TRICKSTER: This is a nice spot. I'm glad I came up here.

COYOTE: It's right along the trail. People ride by on melancholy horses. (*Musing.*) Melancholy horses . . .

TRICKSTER: Uh, what'd you see up there?

COYOTE: Where?

TRICKSTER: In the upper world.

COYOTE: Woodchucks fuckin' in the trees.

TRICKSTER: Outasight. Woodchucks fuckin' in the trees. Outasight.

COYOTE: Yeah. (*Pause.*) Where'd you come from? Originally, I mean.

TRICKSTER *points.* COYOTE *is startled but takes his protective posture.*

TRICKSTER: There! (*Smiles, dropping the point.*) That was some fall. My father fell out of a tree when he was a kid. Hasn't been the same since. At least, that's the story. . . .

COYOTE: I feel strong. I feel strong enough to go on the warpath.

TRICKSTER: Who are you mad at?

COYOTE: You don't have to be mad to go on the warpath. You just go on the warpath. You don't need to make any excuses.

TRICKSTER: (*Offering his hand.*) My name's Smith. (*They shake.*)

COYOTE: Brown. (*Pause.*) What's your personal history? Tell me about yourself.

TRICKSTER: I have no personal history. I've given it up.

COYOTE: What do you do for a living? (*A silence.*)

TRICKSTER: I track people down. I always get my man.

COYOTE *makes a big show of destroying one of his weapons, berating it for being useless and a burden.*

COYOTE: You'll never get Coyote. (*Pause.*) Tell me what's down there.

TRICKSTER: Where?

COYOTE: (*Looking down into the hole.*) In the lower world.

TRICKSTER: It's kinda sandy. Hot. (*Pause. He approaches the hole.*) I don't know, my eyes were closed. Hot. Savage hatred. Anger.

Vengefulness. Helpless . . . I saw tracks. Man tracks. I was coming from a place where the beings had only heads. A voice said: "See. Foot markings. Not the bear. Not the wolf. Where have they come from? Where are they going? See if you can follow." I put my face in the dust and closed my eyes. I felt unarmed, I was vulnerable. I thought, "Who is this man? Where is he leading me?" But I followed the tracks. I am a hunter. I was compelled. It was my fate. . . . I went down, down. I came to a lake. There on the other side of the lake was the man, standing on a buffalo head, pointing at me. The buffalo head was shining white, white as the salt flat, hot white. The man was pointing at me. I looked up. It was the roof of a cave, sky-blue. *"Don't kill me!"* the man shouted. . . .

COYOTE: There! (*Points.* TRICKSTER *protects himself.*) When Coyote goes on the warpath, he goes alone. (*Destroys another of his weapons.*)

TRICKSTER: I don't see how anybody can go on the warpath and be as dumb as you are.

COYOTE: I don't need it. It's just clutter. Useless clutter. That stuff gets in the way, drags me down. I don't need no weapons! When you go on the warpath, you go on the warpath. It's clean! (*Makes a gesture.*)

TRICKSTER: Can you do anything well?

COYOTE: I know plants. I'm a master of plant life. I got things planted around here.

TRICKSTER: What kind of things?

COYOTE: Things to remind me. Plants are voices, messengers to Coyote. They tell him where he is, which way he's going, what's behind him . . . this plant calls to me. He has something to tell me. . . . Yes, little brother? (*Assumes a posture of listening.*)

TRICKSTER *becomes the voice of the plant.*

TRICKSTER: Don't listen to me, Coyote. My tale is a sad one, a story that kills.

COYOTE: Coyote always wakes up again.

TRICKSTER: It is killing to the spirit.

COYOTE: The spirit of Coyote is unquenchable as the waterfall. He is not afraid.

TRICKSTER: The owl never sleeps.

COYOTE: Is that your animal? The owl?

TRICKSTER: When the owl is heard, someone dies.

COYOTE: Coyote can't die.

TRICKSTER: I'll tell you a thing or two, but try not to listen.

COYOTE: Coyote can eat it.

TRICKSTER: My nature is sorrowful. My great Mother weeps, and no one hears. The stars see her distress, but they cannot help her. They are too far away. (OLD SPIDER WOMAN *softly joins in.*)

OLD SPIDER WOMAN AND TRICKSTER: My Mother's hair is torn from her head by the roots. She has steeped her eyes in burning ashes. Her body is swollen, her blood has turned sour. Sharp edges are in her genitals, her breasts bleed, her womb is collapsed.

COYOTE: What have they done!

OLD SPIDER WOMAN AND TRICKSTER: The sun takes pity on her, the moon wobbles in its grief. My Mother's anger is a terrible thing! She longs to tremble, she longs to defecate, she wishes to vomit. She wants to purify herself. But out of compassion, she refrains. Out of charity, she remains still. Out of love, she accommodates herself.

COYOTE: Those assholes! They've pissed on my mother! They've shit in her face! They've poured acid into her liver! They've dumped garbage into her stomach! They've poured filth into her veins, dust into her lungs, disease into the marrow of her bones! Those assholes! Treacherous maniacs! Rip-off artists! Hustlers! Ingrates! Stinking animals! Insensitive beasts! Blind! Selfish! Ferocious dogs! Stupid! Slavish! Ugly, heartless assholes! I'll destroy them all!

TRICKSTER *points.* COYOTE *takes his defensive posture.*

COYOTE: (*Continues.*) My God! I've fallen into my own shit! I didn't mean that . . .

TRICKSTER: I'm a traveling man. I'm a hunter, a stalker, a spy. I've seen that there's no escape. We're in the soup. My stomach is full of bad songs.

COYOTE: I'll tell a coyote tale! One morning Coyote woke up and his blanket was gone. And he looked into the sky and he saw a banner in the sky. He said, "Oh boy, must be feast day. They only fly a banner when it's feast day." So he jumped to his feet. It was then he realized it wasn't a banner at all. It was his blanket on the end of his penis. So he said to his penis, "Little brother, if you keep this up we'll lose the blanket." So he rolled his penis up and put it in a box on his back. And he folded up his blanket and

went on his way. And he came to the shore of a lake and there on
the other side of the lake were women, swimming. And one of
the women was the chief's daughter. Coyote said, "Now is the
opportune time. I will have intercourse." So he sent his penis
across the lake, but as it went it hit the top of the water and made
waves. He brought it back. "No, no, little brother. If you do it
like that you'll scare them." So he took a rock and he put it on the
end of his penis and he sent his penis across the lake but the rock
was too heavy, and he hit the bottom of the lake. So he brought
his penis back and he took the rock off and he put another rock
on and this rock was just right and he sent his penis across the
lake and it went so fast that it hit some of the women and scared
them and they ran for the shore but the chief's daughter was too
slow and the penis went in her. And all the women got fright-
ened and ran to get the men who were strong but they couldn't
get the penis out so they went to the old woman who knew what
to do in matters of this kind. And she recognized him right away.
She said, "Coyote!' And she yelled across the lake, "First born,
come out of there." But of course, he wouldn't. So they went and
got the chipmunk and he chewed the penis into little pieces and
Coyote came from across the lake and he gathered up the pieces
and he went running through the forest throwing the pieces
around and wherever they landed was food! And one piece was
potato and one piece was artichoke and one piece was sharp-claw
berry and one piece was rice. . . . And that is why our penis is
shaped the way it is.

TRICKSTER: Where were you in '68?

COYOTE: Traveling. (*Pause. Quickly does the listening movement related to the plant.*) I was sitting by the waterfall trying to describe
the waterfall
                it was the most lovely waterfall trying to get a grip
on things describe the waterfall
                      in my notebook on the bridge
only goddamn it I have lost my right hand
                    I HAVE LOST MY RIGHT HAND
trying to describe
               the waterfall as it goes
MY RIGHT HAND in the current
                 my head sucking air UP UP
How did I get into the water
I was sitting on the bridge with my notebook
                    in my LEFT hand

as it goes into the water cool and strong flows past
WHERE IS MY RIGHT HAND
                courses through me
                I mean actually courses through me
THE ROCKS
          watch out for the rocks goddamn it
But I have got my head up
              I have got my head up
watch out for the rocks
            MY RIGHT HAND
                 the water is COLD
it has got COLD under the bridge
              deep green cold fast
              nobody knows where it goes
how deep goddamn it
         MY RIGHT HAND
         Has GOD got my RIGHT HAND
Has God got my right hand
Who is God that he should have my right hand
When I am alone in the river
Give me my right hand back God
             I am afraid of these rocks
give me my right hand back God
           there is no God
           there is no right hand
but I need my right hand
         my LEFT hand is busy

even the notebook is gone
        my left hand is busy keeping me in the water
How did I get into the water
How could I go into the water without my right hand
          trying to describe the waterfall
            the SPEED of it
no that is not true
      that is not an accurate description
of the waterfall see the waterfall
        has no TIME in it
     the waterfall has no TIME in it and I must be STILL
therefore I must be still
      if I am still I will get my right hand back
no no

that is not the reason I must be still
                           my LEFT hand
is busy too busy to describe the waterfall
            trying to get a grip on a ROCK
                grab onto a ROCK
if I am still I will SINK
                 no no
that is not the reason
               the water is moving me
I am being moved in the water
                  that is not true either
There is no MOTION in the water
     there is no MOTION in the water
that would not be an accurate description of the waterfall
       to say something about the waterfall
                     with my RIGHT HAND
while the LEFT hand is keeping me up
                  in the water
      busy keeping me up in the water
then the RIGHT HAND

COYOTE *pauses, staring at his right hand.* TRICKSTER *points.* COYOTE *protects himself.*

COYOTE: (*Continues.*) Why have I done this? I have made myself suffer! (*Pause.*) Coyote's right hand fought his left hand for the buffalo meat. . . .

TRICKSTER: Here's a trickster story! Long before people painted their lives onto cave walls, Earthmaker had made earth "just so." People had nothing to worry about. Earthmaker took care of everything. In the morning you opened your window and there was breakfast already made. In the afternoon there was lunch and in the evening, dinner. Everything was "just so." There was no pain, no suffering, everyone smiled and was happy. Everyone, that is, except Coyote-Trickster. He was *bored.* He walked around with a sour face every day. One day when he couldn't stand it any longer, he stopped everything and everybody and screamed, "Why are you so happy? Why do you have those bovine stupid grins on your faces? What is there to smile about? Nothing, *nothing* is happening!" "What do you mean nothing is happening?" the people said. "Nothing needs to happen. Everything is *just so.*" Coyote-Trickster looked up at Earthmaker and howled

"Ahhoooo." "What would you like to happen?" the people asked him. He paused, thought a little and then answered, "I know. What we need here is Death." "Death? What do you mean, Death?" the people said. "I mean Death. The end. Over and out. You put a limit on life and perhaps you assholes start paying some attention to living. Put some meaning into the middle. Stop that stupid grinning." People shrugged their shoulders and went on with their lives, happily smiling as always and soon they'd forgotten the whole thing. Except for Earthmaker who thought, "Uh-oh, there's going to be trouble." A few days or years later there was a footrace and everyone was in it, including Coyote-Trickster's oldest son who was one of the fastest runners. And he was running and running and passing people and he was just about to win when BAMM he stepped on a rattlesnake and keeled over and stopped breathing. This had never happened before so people told him to get up and run. But he wouldn't. So they called Coyote-Trickster and he came and shook him and shook him and said, "Wake up oldest son of mine. This is no time to sleep. This is a time to run and win and bring honor to your family." But he wouldn't wake up or start breathing. It was then that Coyote-Trickster remembered his outburst. So he looked up at Earthmaker and shouted, "Earthmaker, what I said a while back was a joke. I didn't mean a word I said. I was joking. So you just wake my oldest son up and make him breathe again. So he can win the race and bring honor to his family and we forget the whole thing. What do you say, Earthmaker?" (*Pause.*) Earthmaker? (*Pause.*) And since that time there has been Death on Earth.

COYOTE *shows the bag he's been carrying.*

COYOTE: Hoho! You know what this is?

TRICKSTER: No, what is it?

COYOTE: It's a bear bladder. Can you imagine that? When the bear takes a leak, he takes a leak! The bear can out-piss the Coyote any day of the week!

TRICKSTER: What you got in there? You carrying bear piss around with you in there?

COYOTE: You wanna look inside?

TRICKSTER: No.

COYOTE: What I have in here is tiny little children.

TRICKSTER: Oh?

Norbert Weisser as TRICKSTER, *coming out of the earth.*

COYOTE: Right.

TRICKSTER: Who are they?

COYOTE: The sons and daughters of my brothers and sisters. My brother the Silver Fox, my brother the Chipmunk, my sister the Antelope . . .

TRICKSTER: How many of them are there?

COYOTE: A couple hundred . . .

TRICKSTER: What are you doing with them?

COYOTE: If I ever get stuck somewhere with no food, I can eat them.

TRICKSTER: Wily of you.

COYOTE: Right.

TRICKSTER: Show me one.

COYOTE *reaches into the bladder and produces an invisible child.*

COYOTE: You can't see them. They're quite small, and they're not made of flesh, they're made of power. (*Puts it back.*) I suppose you can hardly wait to taste one. Well, you can't have any.

TRICKSTER: Why not?

COYOTE: Your stomach is full of bad songs.

COYOTE *lies down, cradling the bladder, places his silver arrow so that it points out from his anus. He closes his eyes and appears to be asleep.* TRICKSTER *observes him and then advances.*

COYOTE: (*Continues.*) Stay back. This spot is guarded. We've got you covered. My little brother, the asshole, is on the case. One false move and you're in the shit. (TRICKSTER *stops in his tracks. Considers.*) My asshole is the meanest cop this side of the Rockies. (*Chuckles.*)

TRICKSTER: You know, Coyote, I'm hip to where your honey spots are.

COYOTE: Honey spots?

TRICKSTER: You know what I'm talkin' about. I know where each of them spots is.

COYOTE: No you don't. Your sense of smell is dead. Your sense of place is dead. You can't tell one spot from another.

While the COYOTE *suffers,* TRICKSTER *digs up, one by one, a series of small figurines, each accompanied by a specific gesture and sound.*

TRICKSTER: So much for your asshole. They don't call me the Trickster for nothing. See, I watched where you buried your goods. (*Tears come to* COYOTE's *eyes.*) I'm a bounty hunter. I work on a piece basis. And I always get my man.

COYOTE *gets to his feet and angrily breaks his arrow.*

COYOTE: Useless! Useless suffering!

TRICKSTER *approaches him holding the figurines.*

TRICKSTER: These are your honey spots. These are the moments of your buried love. Here are the moments of passion, of sweet affection, of tenderness. Here are the sensations of the body. The deep feelings—joy and pain. The face of the beloved, the voice of the beloved, the beloved as she comes to you, as she opens her arms to you. The kiss of the beloved. Here is your grief at separation. Here also is your fear, your jealousy, your greed to possess.

COYOTE: You thief! You voyeur! You lousy spy! Why don't we stop fucking around and prepare for battle? Coyote and Trickster, one on one.

TRICKSTER: I don't want to fight, I want to eat. I've become a human being. I'm a person and I have to learn how to eat.

COYOTE: Can you eat the food that is prepared for you, Trickster? Look what you have in your hands already. Can you eat? Do you have the stomach? Can you bear it? This is powerful food you got there in your hands, very special stuff, stuff of the spirit.

TRICKSTER *cautiously sniffs, touches the dolls with his lips.*

TRICKSTER: They're made of straw.

COYOTE: You must know how to eat them. Are you a human being?

TRICKSTER *licks them; tries to take a bite.*

COYOTE: Hoho! You want to know what those things are? You know what those are? Ha! When the chipmunk bit off my penis, he buried the pieces here on this spot! You've just been eating my dick! Hoho!

TRICKSTER *flings the figurines away.*

OLD SPIDER WOMAN: Boys, boys... Can you be anything at all? Your tree; your animal, the owl? Can you be blue jay? Can you be Coyote? For ten seconds?

COYOTE: Twenty seconds!

TRICKSTER: To death, Coyote!

COYOTE: Coyote cannot die!

COYOTE *finds a spot and becomes blue jay.* TRICKSTER *points when* COYOTE's *attention wavers.*

TRICKSTER: I'll bring it into your feet! Into the groin! The bowels! The lungs! The head! I'll stalk you to death!

COYOTE: Coyote is immortal! His home is in the upper world, while the Trickster wanders forever in the earth!

TRICKSTER *finds a spot and becomes owl.* COYOTE *points when* TRICKSTER *loses concentration.*

TRICKSTER: No! Not forever!

COYOTE: Forever, Trickster! As long as Earth lives, Trickster lives!

COYOTE *becomes Coyote.* TRICKSTER *points. The battle is over.* COYOTE *takes his posture which he holds until his final speech.*

TRICKSTER: No! I want to get out of my body! I want to go back to the place where the beings have only heads! I don't want to be flesh! I want to be a clean white bone sticking out of the ground! I want to be a dead buffalo head bone! A bone dead structure in the ground! I want to be a line! I want to be a sign, a scrawl, a circle on a rock! I want to be a rock!

COYOTE: You have to get way above the snow line... on the mountain peak. In the sky. Way above the snow line....

TRICKSTER *is trying to crawl back into the earth.*

TRICKSTER: I want to go down! I want to go down into the earth! Into the ground! Down into the center of the earth!

COYOTE *gently restrains him in the twilight.*

COYOTE: No, Trickster. Stay. It's all right. Listen. It's quiet. Look, all around us it is beautiful. Look, we're here—in the middle. (*Gestures.*) The waterfall comes to earth. It's all right. (*He makes the spiraling movement.* OLD SPIDER WOMAN *steps into the space and points.*)

OLD SPIDER WOMAN: There!

COYOTE: It's that old Spider Lady! (*Spits.*) I think I'll go for a run! (*Runs off.*)

OLD SPIDER WOMAN: Coyote has gone running. Let him go. I think he is an idiot. (*Pause.*) I have to send someone on an important mission, Trickster. Someone *big.*

TRICKSTER: Is it very hard?

OLD SPIDER WOMAN: Oh, yes. It is very hard. Only a *great man* can do it.

TRICKSTER: I'll go, then! I'm the only man around who *can* do it!

OLD SPIDER WOMAN: Good. Now I'm going to bring the sky down. It is too far up there.

She "brings the sky down" as TRICKSTER *ducks, assuming his protective posture.*

OLD SPIDER WOMAN: Come on. This part is over now.

TRICKSTER: Right!

He follows her off.

Norbert Weisser (TRICKSTER), *Ellen Blake* (OLD SPIDER WOMAN), *and Darrell Larson* (COYOTE) *on the set at Padua Hills.*

Coyote II: The Shadow Ripens

On Coyote II: The Shadow Ripens

The main approach here was in working with the idea of gravity. We began with exercises exploring the weight of the body, the pull of the Earth. Then we created "gravity holes," places where the pull was lessened or increased. First the actor struggles alone, then is followed and helped, at the right moment, by his partner. Old Spider Woman puts on the "gravity" or takes it off, as she wills. Emphasis was on body weight, its accompanying postures, and on the "weight" of sound.

The story, on one level, is about "one-heartedness." In spite of Coyote/Trickster's helplessness in the face of Old Spider Woman's power, and of his victimization by his own clumsiness, impulsiveness, trickiness, he is always given another chance. In this instance, he must turn to his "good deities" (advice which comes from the Hopi creation myth). We interpret this to mean a pure sound and movement, of necessity new each performance, simple and direct and pleasing to the "Gods": one-heartedness. Old Spider Woman has the option (never employed) of refusing to take off the gravity. In his one-hearted response to the situation, Coyote/Trickster is freed.

A moment later he blames the stars. He will go up there and "fix" them. And he reaffirms his belonging also to the Earth: he decides to "get a job as a buffalo."

Night. A can of Sterno burns in the center of the clearing. OLD SPIDER WOMAN *breaks her repose. She assumes a posture of command and addresses the audience.*

OLD SPIDER WOMAN: First, they say, there was the only Creator, Taiowa. So Taiowa created Sotuknang, to make things manifest, and to help carry out the harmonious plan. (*Proudly.*) Sotuknang went to the universe which was to be the First World, and out of it he created *me,* Spider Woman. When I awoke to life and received my name, I asked, "Why am I here?" "Look about you," said Sotuknang. "Here is this earth we have created, but there is no life on it. We see no joyful movement, we see no joyful sound. What is life without sound and movement?" So I took some earth. (*She scoops a handful, spits into it.*) And I molded the earth into two beings, twins. And one was sound, and one was movement. Naturally, the two little critters sat right up and asked, "Who are we? Why are we here?" (*To her right hand.*) You are here to help keep this world in order! (*To her left hand.*) You are here to send out sound! (*A gong.* COYOTE *is seen and heard way off, running toward us.*) And all the vibratory centers along the earth's axis from pole to pole resounded to the call! The whole earth trembled! The universe quivered in tune! Thus the whole world was made an instrument of sound, resounding praise to the creator of all! (*She looks off.*) Here comes Coyote, running. (*She makes the posture and movement indicating: "fooling around with the gravity."*) Ha! Coyote is known as Imitator, because *he* only does what other people do. (*Scoffing, she returns to her "throne" in the crotch of a tree.* COYOTE *arrives and stops short, announcing:*)

COYOTE: Coyote can run a thousand miles and never get tired! He is never even out of breath! Coyote can fly over the land in leaps and bounds! (*He suddenly starts trying to catch his breath.*) Wait a minute! There's something wrong here! This is a funny place! Someone has been fooling around with the gravity here! I don't like it! (*He breathes fast, resisting the pull of gravity.* SPIDER WOMAN *breathes with him.*) This place is like under water! (*He shouts, defiantly.*) Coyote is great! He has attained life by his own powers! (SPIDER WOMAN *scoffs.*) I know what I'll do! I'll go fishing! (*Winking at the audience, but still struggling with the weight of gravity, he points to a spot and seems to be fishing there.*)

OLD SPIDER WOMAN: (*Breathing intensely.*) The shadow is ripening! The shadow ripens! (*An old buffalo head-bone appears out of the ground, behind* COYOTE.)

COYOTE: I know you're down there, hiding under a rock! You'll make a fine dinner for Coyote!

OLD SPIDER WOMAN: The shadow is ripening! (TRICKSTER'*s head appears under the buffalo head-bone.*) The shadow ripens! (TRICK-STER *squirms partly out of the ground.* COYOTE *wheels about.*)

TRICKSTER: Coyote! Help me out of here!

COYOTE: Hoho! I knew you were coming up over there! I was only pretending over here.

TRICKSTER: Hey, what is this? What's going on here? I think the gravity is bad in this place! I'm having a very hard time of it! Even my bones are too heavy!

COYOTE: Well, what were you doing down there? Nobody told you to go down there.

TRICKSTER: I was sent on a very important mission by Old Spider Woman. Only a great warrior could accomplish such a mission. Do you think I was having fun down there? Look, it has turned my hair white. It was a very hard job!

COYOTE: (*As if under water.*) Tell me about it.

TRICKSTER: Coyote, I don't like the sound of things here. The sound has weight. (*Pause.*) Things are very thick here. (*Pause.*) There is a tribe. They live on a polar ice cap. Things were very clean there for a long time. And then something happened. It got all fucked up. A plague hit that tribe. There were accidents and tragedies and people were sad and they couldn't understand it. They called Spider Woman, and she called me! She knew I was the very man for the job!

COYOTE: Well, get to the main part. We don't have all night.

TRICKSTER: I had to sit on a hill by myself. I had to sing in harmony from that hill. It's not far from this place here.

COYOTE: I know that hill! I leave my scent there! That's one of *my* places!

TRICKSTER: Well, *I* got to join that tribe on the polar ice cap! I knew I had to swim down through the bedrock. I've been that way before. An igloo was built, seal skins covered the walls and the floors. I sat on a high stage. We all got our centers vibrating. We spoke in a language never heard of before, and *I* began.

COYOTE: Let me talk now! I don't know about you, but I have had a great time myself! I have gone running. I ran all around this earth. I saw the holy mountain at the head-bone of the earth. It was next to a magical blue lake. You could look into that lake and see wonderful things—things of the future, things of the past, things of the upper world!

OLD SPIDER WOMAN *intensifies the "gravity."*

TRICKSTER: I think they gave me drugs, those strange people! I thought I was going to die. I was afraid to die! The gravity had changed! The center had changed! I felt fever. I felt trembling. I was falling. My bloodstream was poisoned. The blood was pumping. I heard overwhelming sounds, like earthquake, like thunder.

COYOTE: I saw people who were beasts of burden. I saw them from my high place, where I sing my song. All around me they were building, building. They were making it tough on Coyote. They were beasts of burden building burdens for Coyote and themselves. I could not sing there. I wanted to keep on running. I wanted to run high up into the mountains, high above the snow line. . . . I saw children sitting on railroad tracks, in the snow, very sad . . . they were like sad little warriors in the snow. . . .

OLD SPIDER WOMAN *takes off the gravity a little.*

TRICKSTER: And then I heard the voice of Earth Mother. I knew that I would live. "Balance and breathing," she said, "balance and breathing, and you'll live for sure, Trickster." So I kept on swimming through the bedrock. Then I remembered Old Spider Woman. "Trickster," she said, "when you come to the place of Earth Mother, if there are no children playing, then don't go in there. That means she will be in a very bad mood, and you will never come back. But if there are children playing, then go in, it's all right. Then you will come back, Trickster, back through the bedrock. And it will be hard, but don't give up. You will hear a chant, and the chant is, 'The shadow is ripening, the shadow ripens.' This will help you. So don't be afraid."

COYOTE: It was that Old Spider Woman who fooled around with the gravity! She's made a trap for Coyote. (*Stalking.*) That old bitch is around here someplace! If I catch her, I'll have intercourse with her! I haven't had intercourse in a long time! I've been too busy running!

Fighting the weight of gravity, and oblivious to everything else, COYOTE *continues to search for* OLD SPIDER WOMAN, *slowly getting himself entangled in one of her "webs."*

OLD SPIDER WOMAN: Trickster, I put the gravity on to help you remember. Have you forgotten?

TRICKSTER: Yes . . . No! I was sent to Earth Mother to ask a question.

OLD SPIDER WOMAN: What was the question?

TRICKSTER: When I got to the place of Earth Mother, after swimming very hard and overcoming every obstacle, there were no children playing. I got so scared that I ran away and hid in a cave. I don't know how long I sat in that cave. There was no time in that cave. Then I heard the sounds of children playing and singing, so I came out. But meanwhile, I had forgotten the question. So I said, "Earth Mother, where have all the buffalo gone?"

OLD SPIDER WOMAN: And what did she answer?

TRICKSTER: She said they were in the land of the dead.

OLD SPIDER WOMAN: And when will they return, so that the people can live?

TRICKSTER: In the next world. (*Pause.*)

OLD SPIDER WOMAN: In the next world ... (*As if trying to remember.*) In the First World, the people understood themselves. In his heart man felt the good of life, its sincere purpose. He was of one heart. The first people knew no sickness. But there were those who permitted evil feelings to enter. They were said to be of two hearts. Not until evil entered the world did persons get sick in the body or the head. ... The First World was destroyed by fire. ...

COYOTE: (*Breaking out of the "web."*) Trickster, come out of there and help me find that Old Spider Woman! I want to have intercourse with her!

TRICKSTER: Coyote, come and pull me out and then I'll help you! Earth Mother has scraped away my youth! It is too difficult for me!

COYOTE: (*Approaches, hesitates.*) No! It's a trick! You'll drag me down there into the world of the Ant People!

OLD SPIDER WOMAN: In the Second World, the people built homes and villages and trails. They made things with their hands and stored food like the Ant People. They could see and talk to each other from the center on top of the head, because this door was still open. Everything they needed was on this Second World, but they began to want more. That was when the trouble started. They forgot to sing joyful praises to the Creator and began singing praises to their goods. This world was turned upside down. It stopped rotating and turned to ice.

COYOTE: I had to make a great effort in those days. I had to get the world turning again. I had to turn it right side up and get it rotating again in its proper place.

OLD SPIDER WOMAN AND TRICKSTER: Coyote had nothing to do with it.

COYOTE: And then I brought a message from Taiowa: First, respect me and one another. And second, sing in harmony from the tops of the hills. When I do not hear you singing from the tops of the hills, I will know you have gone back to evil again. (*Pause. To* TRICKSTER.) So you can come out of that Ant hill now.

TRICKSTER: In the Third World they advanced rapidly and built big cities, countries, a whole civilization. They got preoccupied. Some of them had the power to fly through the air on a shield made of hide.

COYOTE: Coyote can do that to this day! Only he don't need no shield!

TRICKSTER: They could fly around and attack one another. So war and corruption came to this world too. That's why the world has to be destroyed once in a while, so we could have a fresh start. This particular world was destroyed by water.

OLD SPIDER WOMAN: I had to save the people who still had the song in their hearts. It was me who saved them. The world was flooded. But to those who still had the song in their hearts, I said, "You must continue traveling on. Your inner wisdom will guide you. The door at the top of your head is open. Just keep your doors open, and your spirits will guide you."

OLD SPIDER WOMAN AND TRICKSTER: The name of this Fourth World is World Complete. It is not all beautiful and easy like the previous ones. It has height and depth, heat and cold, beauty and barrenness. It has everything for you to choose from. It's up to you to carry out the plan of creation. But if you don't want to, I'll start all over again. You will have help from the proper deities, from your good spirits. Just keep your doors open and remember what I have told you.

COYOTE: (*Pounding his head.*) I knew all that already! I knew all that already! I knew all that already! (*Pause.*) I know what I'll do, I'll ask my little sister where that Old Spider Lady is. (*He takes the plant posture.*) Little sister . . . ? (OLD SPIDER WOMAN *steps into the space and challenges* COYOTE *to battle.*)

OLD SPIDER WOMAN: Here I am, Coyote!

COYOTE: Ha! (*He bends over, pointing his anus at her, ready to fire. She kicks him.* COYOTE *falls over, as if dead.* SPIDER WOMAN *steps center stage.*)

OLD SPIDER WOMAN: That sky is too far up there. A person can't see the stars. (*She does "bringing the sky down" movement, causing the strings of Christmas lights in the trees to come on.* COYOTE *wakes up and starts hitting and berating his anus.*)

COYOTE: You stupid anus! You are not my brother! You are a useless weapon! I don't need you anymore. (*Etc. He collapses from the effort, notices the stars.*) I did that! That's *my* work!

TRICKSTER: Old Spider Grandmother, Coyote said that if you would fix the gravity around here, he would have intercourse with you.

COYOTE: I never said that.

OLD SPIDER WOMAN: Well . . . I don't know . . . it takes a lot of power. Earth Mother is not feeling well, her axis is under a lot of strain. And besides, the moon is wobbling . . . but if Coyote will have intercourse with me, I might be able to fix it for a while. (*She makes the "taking off of gravity" movement.* TRICKSTER—*very old—scrambles out of the ground as fast as he can.* SPIDER WOMAN *lies down expectantly.*)

COYOTE: Wait a minute, I'm not ready.

OLD SPIDER WOMAN: Why not? Let's go!

COYOTE: No, you can't rush these things. These are delicate matters. I have to talk it over with my member. (SPIDER WOMAN *sighs impatiently, while* COYOTE *addresses his member.* TRICKSTER *speaks for* COYOTE'*s member.*) Little brother?

TRICKSTER: Yeah?

COYOTE: Are you in the mood for intercourse?

TRICKSTER: No.

COYOTE: I think you'd better get ready. Old Spider Lady is waiting. I think you are too soft now.

TRICKSTER: I'm not in the mood.

COYOTE: I think you should get in the mood pretty quick, or she'll put the gravity back on.

TRICKSTER: I don't care. I'm not in the mood. I think she has sharp stones in there. You better send someone in there with a hammer and chisel.

COYOTE: I don't like the way you're acting. You're going to get me in a lot of trouble.

TRICKSTER: You can't tell me what to do. I am an independent person. I'm not a two-hearts, like some people. If I'm not in the mood, I'm not in the mood.

COYOTE: I'm bigger than you, so you act the way I tell you to, or . . .

TRICKSTER: Or what?

COYOTE: I'll cut you off and feed you to the birds.

TRICKSTER: Go ahead. But I ain't goin' in there. If I go in there, I'll never get out again. (COYOTE *considers.*)

COYOTE: (*To* OLD SPIDER WOMAN.) He won't do it. (SPIDER WOMAN *leaps to her feet.*)

OLD SPIDER WOMAN: I've never been so insulted in all my life!

TRICKSTER: (*With a sigh.*) Woman.

COYOTE: There's nothing I can do. Sometimes he wants to, and sometimes he doesn't. (*She puts the gravity back on.*)

OLD SPIDER WOMAN: Too bad. Now I've no desire anyway. For a minute there I forgot what a dope you are.

COYOTE: (*Temptingly.*) If you take the gravity off, I'll give you a drink of wine.

OLD SPIDER WOMAN: Something stinks around here. (*Referring to the bladder.*) What do you have in there?

COYOTE: It's the wine.

OLD SPIDER WOMAN: What's it made of?

COYOTE: Many dead little children. They're fermented now. I've been running and I forgot them.

OLD SPIDER WOMAN: You are an idiot, Coyote. (*She returns to her tree.*)

COYOTE: Actually, it's made of pure Rocky Mountain Spring Water.

TRICKSTER: I'll have some, I've been working my ass off.

COYOTE: Help yourself. (*They drink.*) Uh, oh.

TRICKSTER: This is good. What's the trouble now?

COYOTE: I feel funny. I forgot that I beat up my anus and threw it away.

TRICKSTER: Boy, that was stupid.

COYOTE: How about you letting me have your plumbing apparatus?

TRICKSTER: What'll you give me for it?

COYOTE: What do you want?

TRICKSTER: I want to be young and strong and feel the urge for intercourse.

COYOTE: Coyote can do that, but the gravity is in the way.

TRICKSTER: Let's fight the gravity and then I'll decide.

COYOTE: I can't fight without my little brother, the anus, my little brother, the large intestine.

TRICKSTER: Okay. I don't need my large intestine. I'm an old man. I'll loan it to you while we fight the gravity.

COYOTE: It's a deal. (*They do the sound and movement indicating "exchange of the large intestine."*) Good.

TRICKSTER: Now let's prepare to fight the gravity.

COYOTE: Yes. We have to ask the gods for help.

TRICKSTER: Let's go, then.

They start to move, but SPIDER WOMAN *has intensified the gravity. They can hardly walk.*

TRICKSTER: I think this is too much work now. We might as well sit down. It'll save a lot of energy.

COYOTE: Right. (*They settle themselves around the can of Sterno.*)

TRICKSTER: That woman is being mean.

COYOTE: I think some women are good for some things, some women are good for other things, and some women are good for nothing. . . . And some women . . .

TRICKSTER: I'm a traveling man myself, I haven't had too much time for women. That's why I want to get the urge back, before it's too late.

COYOTE: Let me enlighten you. I remember, for instance, Emily, from Berkeley. She always wore work shirts and she had the most beautiful breasts I have seen to this day. Heh, heh, her boy friend, who was a very bad sport, slashed my tires. Emily . . . she gave great head.

OLD SPIDER WOMAN: I heard that, Coyote. Watch it.

COYOTE: Margo of Ann Arbor was an interesting person. She appeared at my side while I was practicing running. She stayed with me for two days. She never spoke, but she could have intercourse while running. (TRICKSTER *is amazed.*) Then she looked away for a moment—and there was her ride to the west coast, waiting.

TRICKSTER: While running?

COYOTE: (*Nodding sagely.*) While running. You would have loved Crazy Chrome Faced Woman. She lived in a hut and collected hubcaps. We became good friends. She had the most extensive collection of hubcaps in North America. She was as fearless as Coyote. She could grab a hubcap off a moving car. And Cho Min who sincerely liked men, in fact she trusted them, especially Coyote. . . . But most of all I remember . . . (*Sobbing.*) I remember She Who Could Not Be Named, who was Coyote's one true wife. This woman was impeccable. From this woman, Coyote learned the meaning of happiness. . . .

TRICKSTER: Why are you so sad, Coyote?

COYOTE: This woman, my wife, is in the Land of the Dead now. (*Pause.* COYOTE *is inconsolable.*)

OLD SPIDER WOMAN: Are you crying for your lost woman, Coyote?

COYOTE: Yes. I long for her. There is a great pain in my heart.

OLD SPIDER WOMAN: Coyote, your pain is one-hearted. I have taken pity on you.

TRICKSTER *stands and becomes "Spirit of the Dead."*

TRICKSTER AND OLD SPIDER WOMAN: I can take you to the place where your wife has gone, but you must do exactly as I say. Don't make any foolish mistakes.

COYOTE: Well, what do you expect? Of course, I will do whatever you say!

TRICKSTER: Well, then let's go. (*They start for "The Land of the Dead."*)

COYOTE: I can't see you. You are like a shadow on a dark day.

TRICKSTER: Look at all those horses! It must be a roundup!

COYOTE: (*Pretending.*) Oh, yes! Look at all the horses! (*They continue on.*) Must be a roundup!

TRICKSTER: We're almost there. Your wife is in a long lodge here. Wait here and I'll find out exactly. (*He walks around the space, returns to* COYOTE.) Okay, I know where your wife is. (*They mime "entering the lodge."*) Sit down here by your wife. (SPIDER WOMAN, *enshrouded, has become* COYOTE's *wife.*)

COYOTE: I can't see her. She is like a shadow on a dark day.

TRICKSTER: She has prepared our food. Let's eat. (*They mime "eating."*) Now, you stay here. I have to go around and say hello to some people. (*He goes about pretending to say hello to intimates in the audience, then returns to* COYOTE.)

COYOTE: Spirit of the Dead, I still can't see my wife! What should I do?

TRICKSTER: Listen, and I will advise you. You must travel five mountains to the west. Your wife will be with you. Slowly, the shadow will ripen. But do not yield to some notion you may have to do something foolish. Do not touch her. When you have crossed the fifth mountain, you can do what you want.

COYOTE: That's the way it'll be, then!

COYOTE *rises. His "wife" rises with him and follows. They go back through "The Land of the Dead."*

COYOTE: Look at all those horses! It must be a roundup! (*He looks about for a reply. Silence. He still can't see her. They come back into the space.*)

TRICKSTER: I hope he does everything right, and takes his wife back from the other world. This is the fourth mountain. (*Pause.*) The shadow is ripening... the shadow ripens...

COYOTE *and* SPIDER WOMAN *approach the Sterno. He begins to see her. For a moment he stands transfixed.*

OLD SPIDER WOMAN: Coyote, do not touch me!

But COYOTE *can't help himself and grabs for her.* SPIDER WOMAN, *furious, throws off her shroud.*

OLD SPIDER WOMAN: Coyote! You idiot! You were told not to do anything foolish! We could have established the practice of returning from the Land of the Dead! Now it will never be so! You have ruined it! (*She returns to her tree.*)

COYOTE: No! No! (*Crazed with grief, he races back out through "The Land of the Dead."*) Look at all those horses! It must be a round-up! (*He rushes back into the space. He sits down across from* TRICKSTER *and mimes "eating." He becomes very sad.*)

TRICKSTER: Coyote listened for the voices. He looked all around, but nothing happened. Coyote sat there in the middle of the prairie. He sat there all night but the lodge didn't appear again. In the morning he heard meadowlarks... (*Pause.*)

OLD SPIDER WOMAN: (*Gently.*) Coyote/Trickster, you have done a terrible thing. But your doors are still open. I have compassion for you. You must turn to your good deities with one-heartedness. If you can do this, I will take off the gravity.

Separately and then together, COYOTE/TRICKSTER *approach the deities one-heartedly.* SPIDER WOMAN *takes off the gravity.*

TRICKSTER: (*Quickly.*) Coyote, I'm tired of all this hard work. I've decided to get a job as a buffalo for a while. What are you going to do?

COYOTE: I'm going to the upper world. I think the stars are cruel. I'm going up there to fix them.

TRICKSTER: Well, goodbye.

COYOTE: Good luck, Trickster.

They shake hands. TRICKSTER *runs off.* COYOTE *looks at the sky, then races up into the tree....* SPIDER WOMAN *steps into the space.*

OLD SPIDER WOMAN: This is the Fourth World... (*Sigh.*) ... the World Complete... but Earth Mother has said that things are getting too hard for her.... I'm going to move the sky back up. It's too close now.

She makes the "moving the sky" gesture. The lights go out.

Darrell Larson as COYOTE.

Coyote III: Planet of the Spider People

There are large hairy spiders everywhere—in webs, on the ground, hanging from the trees, etc. Also two large rocks, one with buffalo horns sticking out of it. COYOTE, *distraught, eyes tightly closed, crawls down a tree into the space.*

COYOTE: Trickster! Trickster! Where are you? I'm lost, Trickster! I don't know where I am! (*He inadvertently brushes against something and gets a shock.*) *Ahhhh!* Everything is electrified in this place! Oh, no! Trickster, come up! Come up, Trickster! (*Silence.*) Oh, I'm lost and sad! How did this happen to me? (*Silence.*) Great Spirit! I'm tired of being lost! I'm tired of being sad! I'm tired of being lonely! I can't see! And everything is electrified here!

TRICKSTER *is in the big rock with two buffalo horns.*

TRICKSTER: Hey, Coyote. Stop complaining so loud. You'll wake up all the people.

COYOTE: Who's talking here?

TRICKSTER: Me. You're not the first person who ever had a hard time of it, so stop feeling sorry for yourself and be quiet.

COYOTE: I'll yell if I want to! I'll talk if I want to! I am Coyote! I have come up here to fix the stars!

TRICKSTER: Why?

COYOTE: Because there is too much suffering down there!

TRICKSTER: I wouldn't take it personally. From up here it doesn't look like shit or shinola.

COYOTE: I don't like your attitude! I think I'll kill you! (*He flounders around making threatening noises.*)

TRICKSTER: Hey, Coyote. If you promise to stop making so much noise, I'll tell you where you are.

COYOTE: Coyote knows where he is! Coyote is among the stars! I was on my way to straighten things out up here when some evil, tricky person threw dust in my eyes! I think it was that Old Spider Woman! Otherwise, Coyote would have taken care of things already! He'd have done his task and gone back to his own tribe!

TRICKSTER: Calm yourself, Coyote. If you sit where I tell you, you won't get a shock and you'll find out where you are.

COYOTE: Very well, then. Coyote will sit down.

TRICKSTER: (*Directing him.*) Not there. Over there. Now, dig.

COYOTE *digs, discovers a "Milky Way" candy bar.*

COYOTE: Ah! Food! (*He eats.*) You grow good food around here!

TRICKSTER: I never touch the stuff. It's bad for the teeth.

COYOTE: I like 'em better frozen. But thanks a lot, anyway. Thanks a lot.

TRICKSTER: You're welcome.

COYOTE: I still can't see anything. Tell me what my home country looks like, the planet Earth.

TRICKSTER: We don't call it "Earth" up here. We call it Sakasaka-saka.

COYOTE: What does that mean?

TRICKSTER: Little Blue Mother Turning In Space.

COYOTE: Is my mother's color blue?

TRICKSTER: Most of the time. That's the main impression of her. Blue. And she has a little yellow guy turning with her. He's called Babababababa.

COYOTE: And what does that mean?

TRICKSTER: Little Blue Mother's Yellow Little Kid.

COYOTE: Can you see any of my brothers and sisters?

TRICKSTER: No.

COYOTE: Any human beings?

TRICKSTER: No. (*A sort of telescope protrudes from the rock's "head."*) I see thousands of immense clouds of gas and dust! These are the most massive objects in this galaxy! And these great clouds are held together by their own self-gravity! Each one of these things is worth about a hundred thousand suns!

COYOTE: Where?

TRICKSTER: You can't see them. They don't radiate any light. And nobody knows what's holding 'em up there in the first place. (*The telescope retracts.*) If I were you, I wouldn't strain myself in that direction. I'd use my energy to watch out for the Spider People.

COYOTE: (*Leaping to his feet.*) The Spider People! You got Spider People here?

TRICKSTER: I heard of some Spider People around here talking about killing you.

COYOTE: Oh, no!

TRICKSTER: I'll go and find out what they are going to do.

COYOTE: Okay! Come back soon! (*The rock moves a few inches to the right and all the spiders move.*) Creature? Creature?

TRICKSTER: That was another one, a cousin of mine. But I'll tell you something good. Why do you think the Spider Lady hangs around in a tree? What do you think about that?

COYOTE: I don't know what to think.

TRICKSTER: She holds on to the tree and shuts her eyes and she can see everything over the whole Milky Way. This tree here is Chief of the whole Milky Way. That is why spiders always go on trees.

COYOTE: This is news to me.

TRICKSTER: Do you wish to see everything, or not?

COYOTE: Certainly, I do!

TRICKSTER: Well, keep your eyes shut, hold onto this tree and you will see everything.

COYOTE: I'll try it. (*He touches the tree and gets a shock.*) Ahhhh! You tricked me, Creature! You tricked me! I'll kill you!

TRICKSTER: I forgot a part. I'm sorry. Rub your feet on the ground three times and you won't get a shock. You'll like it very much.

COYOTE *rubs his feet, touches the tree, then leaps into the tree and throws his arms around it.*

COYOTE: Oh, I love this tree! I love this tree! This tree is a true Chief! (*The Spider People move.* TRICKSTER *stands, shedding his rock outfit. He wears a buffalo robe and a buffalo headpiece.*) I can see! I can see over the whole Milky Way! I can see the four elements! I can see the four directions! I can see above and below! I can see the beginning and the end! I can see in the middle! And it is . . . ! It is . . . !

TRICKSTER: Don't open your eyes, Coyote. (COYOTE *opens his eyes. The Spider People move. He howls.*)

COYOTE: Did I see that? Did I see that?

TRICKSTER: What?

COYOTE: (*Jumping out of the trees.*) My brother the Buffalo, are you really there?

TRICKSTER: Where?

COYOTE: Don't be an idiot. This is Coyote talking. Are you in front of my eyes or behind my eyes?

TRICKSTER: That question is too thick for me. I can't understand it.

COYOTE: My brother the Buffalo, are there Spider People here, too?

TRICKSTER: I think there are Spider People here, too.

COYOTE: My brother the Buffalo, is there a creature here with a bad attitude?

TRICKSTER: Coyote, I don't see a creature here with a bad attitude.

COYOTE: My brother the Buffalo, if you are really here too, then let's go back to our own tribe.

TRICKSTER: How will we get there?

COYOTE: I will ride there in the hump of your back.

TRICKSTER: There is no hump on my back here, Coyote.

COYOTE: Then I will ride inside you, Buffalo. I will ride in your entrails.

TRICKSTER: There is no room for you in there, Coyote, because I loaned my large intestine to a two-hearted person.

COYOTE: That was a stupid thing to do. Coyote can't get back to his own tribe now.

Voice of OLD SPIDER WOMAN *is heard from within the other large rock.*

OLD SPIDER WOMAN: Oh, the shame of the eyeballs! The horror of the feet!

TRICKSTER: There is a creature here with a bad attitude.

The Spider People move. COYOTE *and* TRICKSTER *head for the trees.*

OLD SPIDER WOMAN: You see that? You can't make a move around here without stepping on something.

COYOTE: (*Clinging to the tree.*) My brother the Buffalo—who is this guy?

TRICKSTER: Hey, Creature—are you a bona fide Indian or a two-heart white-eyes?

OLD SPIDER WOMAN: What difference does it make? I'm a person!

TRICKSTER: What tribe?

OLD SPIDER WOMAN: Shmohawk.

TRICKSTER: Maybe we know that tribe. Where do they make camp? We could be relatives of yours!

COYOTE: I never heard of that tribe!

OLD SPIDER WOMAN: When I was a Shmohawk down there I never knew what was happening. Sit down, buffalo-head. You're making me nervous.

TRICKSTER: I'm afraid of the Spider People.

OLD SPIDER WOMAN: They won't bother you as long as I'm talking.

TRICKSTER: Keep on talking, Creature.

COYOTE: Keep on talking!

OLD SPIDER WOMAN: Well, we didn't know shit from shinola. Thirty-five miles up and nothing exists down there. There's no surface on the surface. No cities, no mountains, no lights, no freeways. And from here? Just a little blue marble spinning in the light of the sun. (*She stops. Movement from the Spider People.*)

COYOTE AND TRICKSTER: Talk, Creature!

OLD SPIDER WOMAN: I acted like I knew what I was doing. All us Shmohawks did. We thought we knew about the stars and planets and atoms and molecules and galaxies and what everything meant. It's frustrating. You don't know when to watch it, when to leave it alone. You don't know if it's ever all right. It's not your fault, but you're responsible. It is all your fault, but you're too hard on yourself. You're damned if you do, and damned if you don't. I got sent up here with all these Spiders because I'm the type which is afraid of stepping on things. But you can watch it just so long, and then—whoop, you've done it again. (*She pauses. Movement from the Spider People.*) You think oranges are apples and bananas are raisins and democrats are republicans. You try and stop one thing and another starts, worse than before. You pay your taxes, and they audit you. You stop smoking and you bloat up. You give up drinking and you find yourself with a taste for kinky sex. You give up sex and you get manic depressive, laughing or crying all the time. You're too loud or too quiet and your own presence is a torture to yourself or a burden to others. To sum up, I think the worst thing about being a Shmohawk is you have no idea what you're doing, but you have to pay the consequences anyway and then you resent it.

COYOTE AND TRICKSTER: Those poor Shmohawks.

OLD SPIDER WOMAN: And then—Bang! You end up here on the Planet of the Spider People!

COYOTE AND TRICKSTER: Oh, no!

OLD SPIDER WOMAN: Look into my eyes, Coyote/Trickster, and tell me what you see.

They peer.

COYOTE: Your eyes are full of pain, Creature!

TRICKSTER: Your eyes are showing a lot of fear, Creature.

OLD SPIDER WOMAN: It's because I have to stay in here and not move. If I come out of here, I might say something, I might do something, I might step on something. But the real horror of it all is, everything is ordinary. Everything is familiar, everything is just a bad habit.

TRICKSTER: I know exactly how you feel, Creature! A long time ago Coyote and I made a vow to Earthmaker to never even touch a woman again, especially if she was young and beautiful. One day, after prospecting in the mountain canyons for gold we decided to go into town for a drink. It had been raining for weeks and the roads were all mud. When we got into town the stagecoach had just arrived and there in that coach was the most beautiful damsel I had ever laid my eyes on. Long blonde hair, blue eyes, the prettiest smile you ever seen, a blue cotton dress, parasol over her arm. As she was trying to get out of that coach she lifted her dress up a little, like this. But of course she couldn't. The roads were overflowing with mud.

OLD SPIDER WOMAN: Is this conversation nearly over?

TRICKSTER: Well, before I could say bip, Coyote was over there, picked her up and carried her across the muddy road into the saloon, put her down on the bar and bought her a drink. The cowboys were whoopin' and laughin'. I was stunned! I didn't know what to think! I couldn't say a word! I couldn't even drink that night! While Coyote was downing one brandy after another! Days later back at the camp I finally asked him, "Coyote," I says, "Coyote. How could you do such a thing after making a vow to Earthmaker?" You know what he said?

COYOTE: Are you still carrying her? I put her down days ago!

OLD SPIDER WOMAN: That story is too thick for me. I can't understand it.

COYOTE: Try to follow this. One day the Coyote and the Trickster needed a judgment made. So they went to Earthmaker. And Earthmaker made his judgment. But the Trickster did not agree with the judgment. So do you know what he did? He put his shoes on the top of his head and walked out of the room!

OLD SPIDER WOMAN: Hey, Coyote, I think I hear your mother calling!

COYOTE: My brother the Buffalo, I feel sorry for this guy.

TRICKSTER: Watch out, Coyote. This is an old trick. This creature has a bad attitude.

COYOTE: My brother the Buffalo, maybe if we help this creature with a bad attitude, we'll be able to go back to our own tribe. Hey. Creature.

OLD SPIDER WOMAN: What?

COYOTE: You got a sun up here?

OLD SPIDER WOMAN: No, I don't have a wife here. It's better that way. If I had a son, he'd grow up to be just like me.

COYOTE: I didn't mean that! I meant the sun in the sky! When the sun rises, you start all over again! That's Coyote's way!

OLD SPIDER WOMAN: The sun won't rise here for another million years, Coyote. One million years here is one sunrise. (*Pause.*)

COYOTE: I know what I'll do!

OLD SPIDER WOMAN: What's that?

COYOTE: I'll turn myself into a woman and become your wife! That way you can start something new!

TRICKSTER: Wait, Coyote! (COYOTE *turns himself into a woman.*) Coyote turned himself into a woman. He was always doing crazy things like that. That's because Coyote had no limits. When the sun rose on Earth, he started over. He forgot all about it. It was all brand new for him. . . .

OLD SPIDER WOMAN: Hey, Miss Coyote—you are a beautiful woman. You really turn me on. My heart is pounding and my member is pulsing. I can think of nothing but you. I can't live without you. In short, I feel romantic.

COYOTE: That's what they said back in my own tribe. All the young men wanted to marry me. I had to go away from there, because I wasn't attracted to any of those young men. . . .

TRICKSTER: Hey, Coyote—why don't you come into *my* lodge? We'll spend the night fooling around. You'll find it very agreeable.

COYOTE: No! I'm not attracted to you! Besides, my heart belongs to another person. He is different than the rest of you. He is an extraordinary person! He's quite a guy!

TRICKSTER: He can't hunt! He can't fish! And he's afraid of stepping on things. He'll have a lot of trouble making a living.

COYOTE: I don't care. He is very sensitive. And Coyote can go kill a hundred rabbits anytime she wants to. She will do anything for her man!

OLD SPIDER WOMAN: Don't listen to him, Miss Coyote, and come into *my* lodge.

COYOTE: I want to, Mr. Creature, but only if your intentions are honorable. You shouldn't take advantage of an innocent girl.

OLD SPIDER WOMAN: I hadn't intended marriage. But I'm in love, so if that's the way it is, then that's the way it is. I want to have you for my wife, Miss Coyote, because I think you're terrific. I'm pretty shy, though. I don't have much experience in these matters.

COYOTE: Let's get married and have kids, Mr. Creature. I find you extremely attractive, so don't worry about that other stuff. Coyote will show you how it's done.

TRICKSTER: Coyote and the Creature tied the knot and retired to their lodge.... Coyote was a good wife.... (COYOTE *mimes*.) She prepared his food ... she sewed his moccasins ... she fed his horses ... she hunted rabbits ... she washed his clothes ... she decorated the lodge ... she arranged a dinner party for a week from Thursday ... she made his bed, and lay down in it to await her husband ... the Creature was very pleased ... (OLD SPIDER WOMAN *belches*.)

OLD SPIDER WOMAN: Now I'll go in to my wife ...

TRICKSTER: At first Coyote couldn't find the Creature's member, because it was in a funny place, but then she got a shock....

COYOTE: Oh! You're electrified!

OLD SPIDER WOMAN: I'm sorry. I forgot to tell you. Rub your feet three times. You won't get a shock. You'll like it very much.

TRICKSTER: Coyote liked it very much. She got pregnant right away.

OLD SPIDER WOMAN: Thank you, Miss Coyote. You're the first woman that ever cared for me as a person. I feel much better about myself. I don't feel so insecure now. In fact, I feel strong enough to go back down there and try again.

COYOTE: But Mr. Creature, you can't leave now—I am pregnant!

OLD SPIDER WOMAN *stands, shedding her rock costume. She is dressed like a man in suit and tie.*

OLD SPIDER WOMAN: I'm sorry, Coyote, but you knew it wasn't serious. You knew it couldn't last. These things happen. I can't let it ruin my life. I have to get myself together now. I'm gonna clean up my act, avoid entanglements, keep my mouth shut, and try not to step on anything. The Earth isn't such a bad place to live. (*She straightens her tie and exits through the audience trying not to step on anything.*)

TRICKSTER: The Creature went back to being a Shmohawk again.

COYOTE: *Oh! Oh!*

TRICKSTER: Coyote was in labor. But the kids wouldn't come out. Hey, Coyote—it's time to give birth now. You got plenty kids in there.

COYOTE: *Oh!* That's what you get for trying to help a guy out! Coyote was very foolish to fall for that guy! *Oh!* One night of temptation! One night of pleasure! And look what happens to a person! Look what happens! And who is gonna take care of the kids now? *Oh!* Coyote is sorry he became a woman!

TRICKSTER: Hey, Coyote—you're in a fine pickle. Maybe I'll give you a hand getting those kids out.

COYOTE: *Oh!* My brother the Buffalo, if you give Coyote a hand pushing these kids out of me, we will go to all the tribes and tell them what a great guy you are and then they won't kill you for your meat!

TRICKSTER: (*To audience.*) I knew that Coyote would forget all about it, but I decided to help him anyway. Otherwise he would keep on yelling. (*Goes to* COYOTE.) Hey, Coyote—the kids can't come out of there because there's no door there. I'll have to make a door, and then the kids will come out.

COYOTE: *Oh!* My brother the Buffalo—make a door! (TRICKSTER *makes a door.*)

TRICKSTER: Okay you kids—come on out of there! (*Pause. He puts his ear to the door.*) First-born, they won't come out.

COYOTE: My brother the Buffalo, why won't they come out?

TRICKSTER: They don't have any names. They're afraid to come out without a name. If you give them a name, they'll come out.

COYOTE: How can I give them a name if I don't know who they are? I never heard of anything so stupid! When I see how they are, I'll give them a name! (TRICKSTER *puts his ear to the door.*)

TRICKSTER: They say you are the true Chief and Father of their tribe, so you should give them each a name. Then they'll come out.

COYOTE: How many of 'em are there?

TRICKSTER: Twelve.

COYOTE AND TRICKSTER: *Oh!* "Takes It All Back Because He Didn't Mean It." (*A Spider Person runs out of* COYOTE.) *Oh!* "Pretends He Is Thinking Of Something Else." (*Another spider.*) *Oh!* "Looks At His Hand With Profound Interest." (*Another spider.*) *Oh!* "Turns Away To See What's Happening There." (*Another spider.*) *Oh!* "Coolly Denies He Is Angry." (*Another spider.*) *Oh!* "Would Rather Be In New York City." (*Another spider.*) *Oh!* "Says It's Not His Ego, But Something Real." (*Another spider.*) *Oh!* "Wishes He Hadn't Done That." (*Another spider.*) *Oh!* "Does You A Favor." "Never Joins The Circle." "Acts Like He Knows What You Mean." "Certain Things He Can't Agree With." (*Four more spiders run out.* COYOTE *falls back exhausted.*)

COYOTE: *Oh!* (*Pause.*) They got all that stuff from their father. (*He sits up. The spiders all crawl and bounce about.* COYOTE *and* TRICKSTER *scream, rush to the trees and throw their arms around them.*)

COYOTE AND TRICKSTER: Spider Grandmother! Help us get back to our own tribe!

A huge straw model of the figurines in "Pointing" rises from the ground, its eyes flashing. COYOTE *and* TRICKSTER *get a shock from the trees and fall to the ground, cowering in fear.* OLD SPIDER WOMAN's *voice is heard as if coming from everywhere.*

OLD SPIDER WOMAN: Coyote/Trickster, you thought you could climb up here and fix things. That was your shadow talking. I had to throw star dust in your eyes. In this way you got lost and you don't know what's real anymore. You even thought you could become a woman. And so your Earthly Mother is ashamed, First-born, and the stars above are turned cold against you. Earthmaker hopes you have learned a lesson from all this.

COYOTE AND TRICKSTER: But Spider Grandmother, when can I go back to my own tribe? And how will I get there?

OLD SPIDER WOMAN: When the sun rises, Coyote/Trickster. When the sun rises. . . .

COYOTE *crawls into* TRICKSTER's *arms. Darkness.*

On the Creation of The Coyote Cycle

Barry Barankin

Because of the unusual manner in which material for the Coyote plays is generated and collected, West Coast Plays *asked Barry Barankin to record for us his discussion with the author and performers. Barry has a background in collectively created theatre. He is writing his dissertation on Le Théâtre du Soleil, which he has studied in Paris.*

The Coyote Company came to San Francisco in October, 1980, to perform the first three of a projected five- to seven-play Coyote Cycle. The plays and the theatrical elements of Coyote performances all stem from a set of exercises described in the introductory notes to the plays. The focus of these exercises is the power relationship between the human being and the place in the universe that he occupies at any given moment. This tangible connection, felt through one's feet and made manifest through sounds and gestures, is the subject of the discussion below, which took place at the Intersection Theatre during a break in the organized chaos that precedes the opening of a show. Playwright/director Murray Mednick and his three performers—Darrell Larson (Coyote), Norbert Weisser (Trickster), and Ellen Blake (Spider Woman)—interrupted their work on the set and props to go through the exercises and talk about them.

BARANKIN: How long have you been working on the Coyote plays?

MEDNICK: Since 1978. We did the first one that year, the second one in '79, and the third one this year.

BARANKIN: How long did you work on each show before you presented it?

MEDNICK: Six weeks. But we spent a lot of time exercising, aside from working on the show. The exercises are at least as important as the plays.

BARANKIN: Do you anticipate anybody else ever doing these plays?

MEDNICK: Sure, other people could do them. But then it's out of

my hands. What I'm interested in is the process that we work on
them with, keeping this company together and doing it until we
don't want to do it anymore. In the meantime, if other people
want to do it, fine.

BARANKIN: It seems to me that if they were done by anybody else
there would still have to be a commitment to the exercises, to the
process.

MEDNICK: Without the kind of work that we approach the plays
with they become performance pieces, and as performance
pieces they're fine, but they would lack for me the underlying
direction which we have in common and which we developed.

BARANKIN: What underlying direction have you developed?

MEDNICK: Each time these performers do the play they have to do
homage to where the play is coming from, which is not only us.
We get a lot of stuff from the old Indian stories and the space,
and from our work with each other. That can't be forgotten.

WEISSER: That's not to say that there isn't any acting, but there's
something in addition to it. The acting has sort of a Brechtian
quality because some of the characters, as they change, are really
characters that are being taken for a walk by the actors. They're
put on. And then we step out of them at times.

BARANKIN: Are there certain gestures which are clearly set?

MEDNICK: They're set *after* we find them. One of the reasons for
the exercises is to find physical posture because that's part of the
grammar of these pieces. We really get a lot of benefit doing the
exercises, physical things. For example that one that Darrell did
today—that's a jewel. And we'll keep that, we'll use that in one
of the other plays.

(NOTE: The gesture involves putting both arms around the head,
though not touching it, as if one were going to unscrew the lid of
some enormous mason jar, and then violently twisting the arms
and head together. The process of bringing the arms up and
around the head is very slow, but the final movement in the
sequence is quick and sharp.)

BARANKIN: What will you do with it?

MEDNICK: I'm going to let it stew, and I'll have it in mind. I'll see it
as an image. So when I'm writing it'll come up.

LARSON: That's how it happens. Often he'll write something that is
either from our lives or from the exercises. Because he saw it
happen. Or many times a moment will require something, and

he'll say, "Remember that exercise you did yesterday? That would be a good gesture here."

BARANKIN: Is there any time during a performance when the actors are free to put in something that's new, that they're just feeling at the moment?

LARSON: Actually we're required, at the end of the second play, to do a sound and movement that is "one-hearted," as if such a thing were possible. So I wouldn't really call it free; it's a requirement and it can't be planned, or it wouldn't be one-hearted.

WEISSER: And it can't be "performed."

LARSON: It's got to be a genuine attempt to contact the deity, which can be done—you *can* pray.

BARANKIN: Would you ever repeat such a gesture?

MEDNICK: It would be a sin to repeat it.

LARSON: And they're almost impossible to remember. It's easier to try to really do it than to remember.

WEISSER: A gesture is also like a prayer, a set prayer. It happened to me in rehearsal, where something very peculiar happened in a gesture, and we kept that particular gesture. For a while it became a dance at one point in the play, but there were times when all I was doing was the gesture—what had really happened wasn't there anymore. So it became like doing an empty set prayer.

MEDNICK: The physical posture and the physical movement are really grammatical, so if we find the grammar we tend to keep it, because it's suitable to that piece—except in the example that Darrell gave, where they're required to do a new sound and movement. That moment is a very difficult one. Now, it's possible to construct a play where there are many of those moments. I've tried to do that but it's extremely wearing—you have to have a company like Grotowski's where you can work on exercises eight hours a day. I think then it's possible, at least in theory, to achieve a kind of presence in the actor all the time. And then that becomes the play; that *is* the play.

BARANKIN: Do the events in the play prepare you for that moment?

LARSON: The first play, *Pointing,* does particularly, for me.

WEISSER: I feel the same way.

BARANKIN: But since you have to do the gesture at the end of the second one...

LARSON: Oh, I look forward to it; now I can get back to the real heart of the exercises.

BARANKIN: Do you anticipate the gesture before you get there?

LARSON: It's actually kind of surprising when it happens. Generally we're too busy to be thinking ahead that much. And it really comes, in a sense, from left field; it comes from Spider Woman. She says "Hey, I'm going to give you one more chance." Because by then Coyote figures he's eliminated his chances—until the sun comes up.

WEISSER: We did say once that if we don't really do it, she won't take the gravity off. So we would stay in that place forever.

LARSON: It says that in the script.

BARANKIN: But it also says "never invoked."

LARSON: Otherwise the folks might get a little testy.

WEISSER: There is something in addition though to those places where we have to do these true moments, and that is an attempt to keep it *all* true. This means, "Don't get lost in the words and in the characters; pay attention to the energy that comes through your feet—all the time, all the time. The moment you lose it, the moment you're thinking of something else, get in your feet."

MEDNICK: It's a superhuman task.

LARSON: But you can always come back to it, because your feet are always there.

BARANKIN: This presents an interesting problem, particularly in *Pointing*. The pointing occurs, one assumes, when you drop the concentration, when you lose that focus. And yet obviously the pointing is set in performance.

LARSON: No, it's not always set. We're required to do an animal. Some of the pointing is in the script but at the end there is an actual battle of concentration, and the moment in which the other person points ... you just do a bluejay until the other person says "Your bluejay just flew away." So those are real exercises. Also, I've always had the sensation that the pointing that is set is for the audience. "You were just gone, weren't you?" Because there's got to be someone in the audience who was gone, and who is alerted by that. He comes back and asks what is actually happening here.

BARANKIN: How is the audience to understand that pointing means you lost your concentration?

MEDNICK: It doesn't have to mean that for them, but my feeling is that it will be clear in the chest. It may not be clear in the head to the audience, but there is a real power that's created by that kind of effort, and it's on the stage—invisible—but it's real. So even if it's not understood by the head it is understood somewhere.

LARSON: It's clear that these guys are having some kind of battle, and they're stalking each other, and looking for a chink.

BARANKIN: In Kabuki there are gestures that are traditional and that have certain set meanings; and the audience knows those gestures. These gestures—the defensive postures and the points —seem to have that same kind of universal constant in terms of their meaning. Would it be better for the audience to know the meaning of these gestures before watching the plays?

MEDNICK: Yes. We're developing a physical language.

BARANKIN: Do you feel as though you're trying to teach a language to people?

MEDNICK: No, I feel like we're creating a physical grammar for these pieces. We know when it's appropriate, because we find it organically. We hope that the language we're finding is a communicable one.

BARANKIN: Outside the plays themselves?

MEDNICK: Yes, it has to be. If you do the exercises right, you can't lie about it. Chances are you'll find a posture that is understood. And at the same time you find a Coyote, and a Trickster, so they're also personal but they communicate.

BARANKIN: The emphasis in the second play, at least in terms of the story, is Trickster's voyage down below. And then in the third one it's Coyote's voyage to the Spider Planet up above. Was there a conscious effort to balance the levels of the worlds in these plays?

MEDNICK: The balance is there, though I may not have done it consciously.

WEISSER: They're the same guy, a being on a journey.

LARSON: Trickster went into the bedrock while Coyote circled the planet. They meet and then go away. They can't both be at the same spot at once, because they can't both be a being: only one can be the being.

BARANKIN: At any given time.

LARSON: But if they could finally come to some peace with each other then maybe a human being would result.

BARANKIN: Can that happen?

MEDNICK: I think that will be a result of completing the mythological cycle. In a way I see it as a development of a certain ease or balance. When that is achieved it will end the cycle. We'll go on to something else.

WEISSER: It's all a moment of harmony. It doesn't have to be for-

ever. If the actors end it in a moment of harmony then they've
clearly won.

BARANKIN: I noticed at one point in the exercises you were doing
earlier you achieved a kind of tense but balanced position, which
was unusual. Usually one person was finding the spot and the
other was pointing at him; there was always a disproportion in
the exercise except at that one point. It seems as if the actors are
making an effort to find moments where they actually are balanced.

MEDNICK: Definitely. And they know it and I know it when it
happens. The exercises can become finer and finer and finer, the
more they work and the more they elaborate on them.

WEISSER: Even the pointing is a moment of balance. It's very short
and it has more of an aggression to it than when we help each
other build something that is long and slow and has more body
to it, but it is a quick moment of being in balance with each
other.

BARANKIN: If you realize you've lost your concentration, don't you
anticipate the point?

MEDNICK: Yes, that's one of the problems in the exercise that the
actor has to work against. Because of that anticipation, and because there is violence in the point—there is somebody stalking
somebody—your only hope is to be really concentrating. You
have to do your work, and then you're safe.

LARSON: During that exercise neither one of us quite had enough
to keep it going but we kept giving back and forth so that we
could keep going as long as we did.

BARANKIN: What happens if one person believes he is totally focused and the other person points at him?

MEDNICK: We talk about it.

BARANKIN: But the response to a point is to go into the defensive
posture, no matter what?

WEISSER: Yes, it is, but I thought about that today. I thought, "If
I'm really focused I don't need any protection."

BARANKIN: Exactly.

MEDNICK: But then you'd have to be strong enough to resist. It's
an interesting proposition. Easy enough to say, but . . .

WEISSER: Usually one is insecure enough to just accept the point.

LARSON: The point itself is such a shock that it knocks you off. And
there are times when, even if you did sense a gap, there's no
space between the exercise and the point; that's just the next

move. Whereas sometimes the point will come and I won't know where I was. And then I really do have to take a defensive posture just to stay standing up. Because I wasn't there.

BARANKIN: Except that if you're really there in your gesture and he points at you, it's the point that's the intrusion and then you have to adjust to *it*.

LARSON: You point when you sense you could get through.

WEISSER: It has happened. I've fallen on my ass. I've been so into a movement that the point . . . I didn't even know where to put my hands, I literally got knocked to the ground. Pure concentration, the kind of concentration that we're after, includes everything, including the defensive position. In other words, if you lose yourself so completely in one thing, then you're not paying attention to everything. There is a stalker outside. Someone is there to point at you, and you need to be aware of him.

MEDNICK: And the space.

BLAKE: Like when Spider Woman comes in at the beginning and scares Coyote out of the space; he has to go running, has to leave the space. He can't be around her.

BARANKIN: Where there are places, which are places of power, and you really feel protected by the spot and by your connection with it, it would be interesting to see if a person could feel so protected by that spot and gesture that he could resist the point, which is a formidable weapon.

MEDNICK: That would be something to try to find out.

WEISSER: There are different levels of just finding the spots. It once happened to me that I had a real strong physical sensation like water hoses at my heels pouring water through my knees into my groin, up through my body. Out of it came a movement. Immediately when that happened I pointed at myself and said, "Oh, my shit! God, what's happening?" And then of course it was gone. So we kept that movement because it was absolutely true; it was like I didn't do the movement, I was "done." But you usually point at yourself because you're so shocked.

BLAKE: This being able to resist a point seems very interesting because you could apply it in a life situation. You would have to be so attuned, your feet would have to be so planted, that someone could come along and either verbally or physically try to knock you off and you couldn't be moved away.

MEDNICK: You'd be so open, so fluid, that it would go right through you.

WEISSER: That's it! That's the Zen concept—an arrow goes right through you, and you let it. And it's no big deal.

BARANKIN: That's what you're talking about too, because if you achieve that kind of openness then when that water comes up to you it doesn't blow you away. You simply say, "Oh, look at this, this is interesting." And it's acceptable to you to have things like that happening.

WEISSER: That comes out of repetition I think, like learning how to swim. But Murray is right: to achieve that with any workable frequency you'd have to have a company like the Polish lab.

MEDNICK: But that can be attained. We're getting something by stretching it out over a period of time, so that it includes all the rest of our lives. Over a long period of time this thing will become very refined and it will be unique to this little company of actors.

BARANKIN: How much time do you spend per day or per week?

MEDNICK: It varies. I like to exercise in the morning and rehearse in the afternoon.

BARANKIN: But do you spend all day at it?

MEDNICK: When we're all together. None of us makes a living at this. It would be ideal if we could take six months and just work on this.

WEISSER: But there is memory. It is a language that you can come back to quicker and quicker.

BARANKIN: How about gestation?

MEDNICK: That's one of the gambles we take. Sometime this year I'm going to write at least one other play. That will come partly from the Indians and partly from me and partly from working with the actors and partly from everything we did before. But I don't know this for sure. It does take a certain amount of cooking.

WEISSER: It has happened that one of the actors comes in and says, "You know what happened to me last night..." and he tells some incredible story and two months later, there it is in a play.

MEDNICK: And that's happening with the new one. I got a story from Norbert that I want to use, I got a posture from Darrell (I saw him walk a certain way), I got an idea about Ellen as a bag woman, and somehow or another all of these things will come together to make the fourth play.

WEISSER: It does stew well. You can use the exercises anywhere: while waiting in a bank, try to be in your feet. By the time you're halfway in your feet you're up at the teller.

BARANKIN: Do you feel committed to the process—the exercise leading to finding things you want to keep, which leads to the writing, and so on?

MEDNICK: It doesn't matter which comes first. Sometimes the writing comes first; each element helps the other. Whichever way we approach it is going to influence every other way we approach it. And they all help get the thing on. We're clearly evolving a way of presenting plays. We work on exercises in such a way that we develop sensitivity to the "spiritual geography" that we put ourselves in.